Systemic Approach to Categorizing and Modeling Requirements

In memory of my dear mother, Batoul, whose love and pride is with me every day.
To my dear father, Habib, whose wisdom is my greatest inspiration.
To my wife, Asma, for her unwavering support.
To my children, Mohammed, Habib, Meriem and Batoul, the true gems of my life.
May this book be a tribute to my family and all my friends.

Series Editor
Jean-Charles Pomerol

Systemic Approach to Categorizing and Modeling Requirements

Azeddine Chikh

iSTE

WILEY

First published 2025 in Great Britain and the United States by ISTE Ltd and John Wiley & Sons, Inc.

ISTE Ltd
27-37 St George's Road
London SW19 4EU
UK

www.iste.co.uk

John Wiley & Sons, Inc.
111 River Street
Hoboken, NJ 07030
USA

www.wiley.com

Library of Congress Control Number: 2025933056

British Library Cataloguing-in-Publication Data
A CIP record for this book is available from the British Library
ISBN 978-1-83669-007-8

Contents

Introduction ix

Part 1. Literature Review 1

Chapter 1. Case Study 3

1.1. E-commerce 3
1.2. Web application for an e-book distributor 4

Chapter 2. Concept of Requirements 7

2.1. Requirements. 7
2.2. Statements of requirements 10
2.3. Goals 10
2.3.1. Nature and definition of goals 10
2.3.2. Benefits of goals 12
2.3.3. Sources of goals 13

Chapter 3. Existing Scales of Requirements 15

3.1. "User–system" scale 15
3.1.1. User requirements 15
3.1.2. System requirements 16
3.2. "System–software scale" 16
3.2.1. System requirements 17

3.2.2. Software requirements 17
3.2.3. Relationships between system requirements and software requirements 18
3.3. "Goal–design" scale 19
3.3.1. Goal-level requirements 19
3.3.2. Domain-level requirements 19
3.3.3. Product-level requirements 19
3.3.4. Design-level requirements. 20
3.4. Discussion 20

Chapter 4. Existing Taxonomies of Requirements 21

4.1. "Requirement–domain property–assumption–definition" taxonomy 22
4.1.1. Requirement. 22
4.1.2. Domain property 22
4.1.3. Assumption 23
4.1.4. Definition 23
4.2. "Faceted" taxonomy 23
4.3. "Behavioral requirements–non-behavioral requirements" (BNB) taxonomy 26
4.4. "Fundamental categories–secondary categories" (FS) taxonomy 27
4.4.1. Fundamental categories 27
4.4.2. Secondary categories 28
4.5. "Functional requirements–non-functional requirements" (FNF) taxonomy 28
4.5.1. Functional requirements 28
4.5.2. Non-functional requirements 29
4.6. Other taxonomies 40
4.6.1. "Primary requirements–derived requirements" (PD) taxonomy. 40
4.6.2. "Business requirements–technical requirements" (BT) taxonomy. 41
4.6.3. "Product requirements–process requirements" (P2) taxonomy. 41
4.7. Discussion 42

Part 2. SMART: A Systemic Approach to Categorizing and Modeling Requirements . . . 45

Chapter 5. Conceptualization . . . 47

5.1. A new reference framework . . . 47
5.1.1. Dimension 1: requirements subjects . . . 48
5.1.2. Dimension 2: requirements factors . . . 56
5.2. New requirement definition . . . 59
5.3. New scales and taxonomies of requirements . . . 59
5.3.1. "User–analyst" (UA) requirements scale . . . 60
5.3.2. "Business–system–software" requirements scale . . . 62
5.3.3. "Endogenous–exogenous" requirements taxonomy . . . 67
5.3.4. Requirements taxonomy by nature . . . 72
5.4. New hybrid requirements categorization . . . 74

Chapter 6. Operationalization . . . 79

6.1. New requirements metadata model . . . 79
6.2. New requirements model . . . 88
6.2.1. Endogenous requirements . . . 92
6.2.2. Exogenous requirements . . . 99

Chapter 7. Usage . . . 107

7.1. Objectives . . . 107
7.2. Usage scenarios . . . 108
7.2.1. Elicitation activity . . . 109
7.2.2. Specification activity . . . 109
7.2.3. Analysis activity . . . 110
7.2.4. Validation activity . . . 111
7.2.5. Qualification activity . . . 111

Chapter 8. Evaluation . . . 113

8.1. Comparison with Somerville's approach . . . 113
8.2. Comparison with Lauesen's approach . . . 115
8.3. Comparison with Robertson's approach . . . 115
8.4. Comparison with Van Lamsweerde's approach . . . 116
8.5. Comparison with Glinz's approach . . . 117
8.6. Comparison with Meyer's approach . . . 117

Conclusion 121

Appendix. Cards Relating to the Nomenclature of the Categories of Requirements 123

References 171

Index 175

Introduction

The increasing technological dependency of the business sector requires that investment in technical systems, and mainly in software, meet their expectations. As software is a strategic tool for these companies, it is imperative that they function in accordance with their requirements. Consequently, the importance of software requirements has increased for these companies and has become a means to anticipate which solutions they should adopt. As such, before implementing future software programs, priority should essentially be given to interpreting and understanding the objectives, needs and preferences, and even the beliefs of these companies (customers) and end-users.

Software development involves at least as much communication as computer science, but educational curricula and project activities are often more concerned with computer science rather than communication. It is sometimes not possible to understand that requirements elicitation is mainly a challenge of human interaction that is not yet automatable (Wiegers and Beatty 2013). Problems often inherent to the difficulty of interpreting and understanding needs, and translating them into well-specified requirements, are behind the cancellation of software projects.

Requirements analysis is a critical task in software development, which first requires studying the scope of the problem, with a view to developing a better understanding of the true goals, needs and preferences of customers and end-users. Unfortunately, many software developers, sometimes well versed, still struggle to understand, specify and manage software requirements. In addition, many users either do not want to express their real needs (retention problem), or cannot do so (communication problem), or they do not know how to do it (incompetence problem).

Although requirements were partially neglected in the former era of software engineering, they have received greater attention in recent decades. Software requirements engineering has actually become its own field of knowledge with its own stakeholders and activities but also with its own concepts, techniques, tools and methods. It can be defined as a coordinated set of activities for exploring, evaluating, documenting, consolidating, revising and adapting the objectives, capabilities, qualities, constraints and assumptions that the future system (system-to-be) should comply with, relative to the problems posed by the existing system (system-as-is) and the opportunities that new technologies make possible (Van Lamsweerde 2009). Its importance mainly stems from the role played by good requirements in achieving any successful software. However, although research in the field of requirements engineering is currently very active, it is still a long way from reaching state-of-the-art maturity in software engineering. The latter has a very long history compared to the former. The dominant trend in software engineering research has been to abstract programming constructs up to the requirements level, rather than propagating requirements abstractions down to the programming level (Mylopoulos et al. 1999).

The first step that we take toward changing this situation in requirements engineering is based on carrying out a diagnosis of its main causes. We actually consider that the current categorizations of requirements, which constitute the backbone of requirements engineering, suffer greatly from ambiguity and lack of coherence. To date, according to Broy (2018), a well-defined requirements categorization is still one of the inadequately solved challenges of requirements engineering.

We believe that this inadequacy is mainly due to the absence of a reference framework for the definition of software elements and the software environment to which the requirements refer. In fact, given the enormous complexity of modern software programs, we believe that it is impossible to properly identify and categorize their requirements without a thorough understanding of the following elements:

– software and its development and operation environments:

- software: composed of functions, data, user interfaces and technical interfaces,

- necessary development environment: consists of the human support (developers), with two types of support, software and hardware – the procedural support for its development (development activities) and the cognitive context of its development (methods, techniques, artifacts and tools),

- necessary operation environment: consists of the human support (end-users), with two types of support, software and hardware – the procedural support for its operation (operation activities of the encompassing system) and the cognitive context of its operation (concepts, goals and rules);

– factors that affect software as well as its development and operation environments:

- quality factors such as usability, reliability, safety and portability,

- compliance factors to the various technological, economic and cultural constraints.

We are thus proposing a new systemic approach to categorization and requirements modeling, named SMART (Systemic Approach to caTegorizing and Modeling Requirements), which takes into account the previous elements to provide the following:

– at the conceptual level:

- a new R2F (requirements reference framework) framework, which makes it possible to precisely define all aspects related to the software and to its development and operation environments; these latter constitute the subjects of requirements as well as the quality and conformity factors that affect them. This framework provides a solid and necessary foundation for all of the following elements. Our hypothesis is that these other elements cannot be established in a systematic way without a logical and common frame of reference,

- a new definition of requirements based on R2F,

- a new hybrid requirements categorization, combining several taxonomies and scales, based on R2F;

– at the operational level:

- a novel requirements metadata model, grounded in RML (requirements metadata language) (Chikh 2017), enables the qualification of requirements using multiple predefined metadata categories,

- a new multi-view requirements model for representing all possible categories of requirements.

Both of these models are based on R2F and on hybrid requirements categorization of the conceptual level.

This book has allowed us to capitalize on our long-term hybrid experience in order to share it with our readers. It thus represents the culmination of no less than 20 years of experience; on the one hand, in the academic world, through master's and doctoral courses (courses in software engineering and information systems and more particularly in software requirements engineering), the supervision of numerous doctoral theses and research projects as well as the publishing of several research articles on requirements engineering-related topics; on the other hand, in the industrial world, through software and information systems development studies and projects, namely for national and international design offices, ranging from analysis and design to implementation and testing.

The book is intended for readers with various profiles and needs: (1) researchers and graduate and undergraduate students in software engineering or related fields such as information systems, Business Process Management (BPM) and Business Process Reengineering (BPR) to further develop their theoretical and practical knowledge of requirements; (2) developers such as analysts, designers, programmers and testers to be used as a guide in their software programming projects; (3) customers and end-users to better understand and be understood by developers; and (4) all interested readers, both novices and experienced, in order to satisfy their scientific curiosity about software requirements. Finally, the author assumes a minimum prerequisite for reading this book, recommending that the typical reader most likely has followed basic teachings in software engineering and/or information systems, or worked on a real requirements project.

This book consists of two main parts. After this introduction, the first part is dedicated to a literature review and comprises the following four chapters: the first chapter presents a case study; the second chapter defines the concept of requirement as well as other underlying concepts; the third chapter presents the scales of the requirements levels; and the fourth chapter presents the requirements taxonomies. The second part is dedicated to the new SMART approach and comprises the following four chapters: the fifth chapter which is dedicated to the conceptualization of this approach by proposing a new requirements reference framework called R2F, and the new hybrid categorization that results therefrom; the sixth chapter is dedicated to operationalization of this approach by proposing a requirements metadata model and a multi-view requirements model; the seventh chapter presents how this approach can be used through different scenarios; and the eighth chapter presents the evaluation of this approach by comparing it with existing approaches. Finally, the conclusion recalls the essential contributions of SMART and opens up some perspectives.

Although one is supposed to follow the order of the eight chapters while reading the book, readers should know that they are free to read it as a whole or in part, in any order, according to their needs and preferences.

PART 1

Literature Review

1

Case Study

The purpose of this chapter is to present a case study relating to B2B (business to business) e-commerce (EC) applied to books that will be used as a basis for the examples presented throughout this book. The online bookstore is a realistic case, easy to understand and fairly representative of software projects. We found inspiration in the features of existing software in this area.

1.1. E-commerce

E-commerce refers to transactions carried out electronically (Turban et al. 2015). EC is a major product of digital technologies, which enables the digitalization of products, services and information. It can be complete or partial depending on the physical or digital nature of its three main activities: orders and payments, order fulfillment and customer delivery.

The main motivation behind EC is its ability to provide companies with a strategic advantage that is essential for them to be more competitive. They can integrate distant and global markets to buy and sell at better prices and thus increase their profits. They are able to accelerate time to market to acquire a competitive advantage. They can improve the internal and external supply chain, as well as strengthen collaboration.

EC is hampered by resistance to new technologies, fear of being defrauded, integration with other IT systems which can be challenging, costly execution of orders, the confidentiality problem, the issues that rather vague regulations create, lack of trust in technology and unfamiliar business partners, difficulties in justifying the initiatives of EC and the lack of skilled labor in EC.

Although the order fulfillment process varies from seller to seller and product to product, it typically includes the following steps: payment and inventory verification, preparation for delivery, contacting customers and returning defective products.

The reformulation of this process through:

1) simplification of the supply chain through coordination between its different stakeholders;

2) more accurate inventories;

3) integration of new information technologies (Radio-Frequency IDentification (RFID), Electronic Data Interchange (EDI), extra-nets, etc.);

will enable it to be more profitable.

Among the main types of EC transactions, we find B2B, B2C (business to customer) and C2C (customer to customer).

Ignoring the laws does not make e-sellers immune to a lawsuit or an accusation that could adversely affect their relationships with customers. One of the most controversial areas of EC is in solving international legal problems. International trade organizations strive to reduce trade barriers in areas such as price regulation, customs, tax issues and regulations on product specifications.

1.2. Web application for an e-book distributor

In order to clarify the new SMART approach and make it more realistic, we look into a case study relating to B2B e-commerce. The wholesale operation of an e-distributor to retail booksellers is the main focus. This case study will serve as a basis for all the examples employed in this book.

Publishers can sell directly to booksellers if the latter are large buyers. However, they generally prefer to use intermediaries (distributors) to distribute their books to large numbers of booksellers. E-distributors collect information about hundreds of thousands of books published by different publishing houses in their catalogs. While most of them sell at fixed prices, others offer quantity discounts, negotiated prices or organize auctions.

The chosen case study refers to a project to develop a new application, called "e-lib", for selling books online to booksellers, through a (fictitious) e-distributor named "mylib". The latter buys scientific books from publishing houses and then resells them to retail booksellers through an online store.

Implementing the "my-lib" online shop of the book e-distributor requires the construction of its website (application showcase), where the books are sold, and its integration with other existing information systems, such as "front-end" for taking orders and "back-end" for the execution of these orders. The store relies on an infrastructure supported by:

1) the employees responsible for its operation;

2) public policy and technical standards;

3) marketing and advertising;

4) security and payment logistics;

5) business partners (banks, insurance companies, tax authorities, etc.).

The online store includes the most common tools, namely, an electronic catalog, which can also be personalized by booksellers and allows them to achieve efficient purchases; a search engine that helps booksellers to quickly find books in the catalog; an electronic shopping cart to store the selected books until payment; electronic auction features to liquidate surplus book stocks; a payment gateway through which payment arrangements can be made; a delivery center where delivery arrangements are made; a customer relationship management (CRM) and partner relationship management (PRM) center. The key to user-friendly navigation for booksellers on the e-distributor's website is to provide a mental map of a potential bookseller. Purchase decision support also includes tools such as comparison agents, recommendations, trusted verification sites and social networks, such as blogs and wikis. These are used for advertising to customers and for collaboration with partners.

The "mylib" e-distributor wants to replace its existing (fictitious) Windows application, called "win-lib", with the new web-based application "e-lib" to ensure more efficient and more profitable online sales to a wider range of customers. The content of the specifications has been intentionally enhanced in order to cover the wide variety of requirements offered by the new SMART approach.

2

Concept of Requirements

The purpose of this chapter is to define the notion of requirement and the underlying concepts. Developed by eminent academics and technicians, the definitions reflect the different points of view of the two antagonistic worlds of theory and practice.

2.1. Requirements

According to Westfall (2014), requirements can be defined as the "what" of a software product. They must be determined and approved by customers, users and suppliers of a software product before building the software.

According to Hood et al. (2008), a requirement is a statement identifying a capability, a physical characteristic or a quality factor that delineates a need for a product or process for which a solution will be sought.

Somerville defines the requirements for a system (in the sense of software) as the descriptions of what it is intended to do, the services it provides and the constraints of its operation. These requirements reflect customers' needs for a useful system, such as controlling a device, placing an order or searching for information. According to Somerville, the term "requirement" is not used harmoniously in software development projects. In some cases, it designates an abstract, high-level statement of a system service or constraint, and in others it represents a detailed formal definition of a function of the same system (Somerville 2016).

In the following, Davis (1993) explains the reason for this difference:

> If a company wishes to let a contract for a large software development project, it must define its needs in a sufficiently abstract way that a solution is not predefined. The requirements must be written so that several contractors can bid for the contract, offering, perhaps, different ways of meeting the client organization's needs. Once a contract has been awarded, the contractor must write a system definition for the client in more detail so that the client understands and can validate what the software will do. Both of these documents may be called the requirements document for the system.

The IEEE 1220-1998 standard defines a requirement as a statement that identifies an operational, functional or design characteristic or constraint of a product or process, that is unambiguous, testable or measurable, and necessary for the acceptability of the product or process by consumers or internal quality assurance guidelines.

Every requirement aspect in this definition is explained by Hull et al. (2017) as follows:

– Statement: although this term rather brings forward the textual expression of a requirement, the latter can also be represented in the form of a table such as Planguage (Gilb 2005), a diagram such as those in UML (OMG 2003), a formal notation such as Z (Spivey 1989), VDM (Jones 1986), LOTOS (Paterno and Faconti 1992), B-method (Abrial 1996) or domain-specific notations (Chaochen et al. 1991). The essential thing in this aspect is to have a traceable and manageable entity, identified as a requirement.

– Product or process: comprehensive solutions include both products (objects built in response to requirements) and processes (procedures for the use of built objects). Requirements can therefore define both the process and the product. In addition, other requirements establish how the product should be developed, usually for quality control purposes.

– Operational, functional or design characteristic or constraint: there are many different types of requirements. Design characteristics cover performance, usability, safety, maintainability and many other qualities.

– Unambiguous: a requirement must lend itself to a clear and unique understanding that is common to all parties concerned.

– Testable or measurable: requirements are used to test whether the design or solution is acceptable. To this end, the requirement must be quantified, thus providing a means of "measuring" the solution against it.

– Necessary for the acceptability of the product or process: this highlights the multidimensional role that requirements play. They will be used to define what needs to be designed and developed, and also to define how the solution should be tested and accepted. They influence the early stages of the development process as well as the later stages during consumer acceptance or internal quality assurance directives: requirements originating from many sources, such as, but not limited to, customers, regulators, users and internal quality procedures.

The famous IEEE 610.12-1990 standard defines a requirement as (1) a necessary condition or functionality for a user to solve a problem or achieve a goal; (2) a condition or capability that must be fulfilled or that should be present in a system or system component to satisfy a formally mandated contract, standard, specification or other documents; or (3) a documented representation of a condition or capability as in (1) or (2).

Consequently, the requirements include not only the needs of users, but also those arising from general organizational, government and industry standards. Clearly, a requirement is a set of needs expressed by the user and various other stakeholders (general organization, community, government agencies and industry standards), which must all be met. Ideally, the requirements are design independent, showing "what" the system should do, rather than "how" it should be done. However, this is not always possible in practice. That is, the meanings of "what" and "how" are different from person to person (Davis 1990).

Other synonyms of the term "requirements" that are used in the real world are needs, constraints, expectations and aspirations (Hull et al. 2017).

Robertson and Robertson (2013) define a requirement as something that the product must do to support its owner's activity, or a quality that it must have to make it acceptable and attractive to the owner. A requirement is created, either because the type of product requires specific functions and qualities, or because the customer rightly demands that this requirement be part of the delivered product.

Laplante (2018) states that the distinction between requirements and goals is a real challenge, mainly for clients and to a lesser extent analysts. According to him, a misunderstanding between the two will have very serious consequences. In fact, on the one hand achieving the goal will be difficult to prove and, on the other hand, the goals evolve as stakeholders change their minds and define goals with behavioral requirements. Laplante proposes to consider a goal as a high-level objective of a company, an organization or a system and a requirement as a specification of how the future system ought to achieve this goal.

2.2. Statements of requirements

Van Lamsweerde (2009) distinguishes between two types of statements: "descriptive" and "prescriptive".

Descriptive statements express the properties of the system that are valid regardless of system behavior. Such properties usually hold due to a natural law or a physical constraint. Descriptive statements are in the indicative mood.

Prescriptive statements express desirable properties about the system that may or may not hold, depending on how the system behaves. Such declarations must be implemented by the system components. These are in the subjunctive mode.

The distinction between descriptive and prescriptive statements is essential to requirements engineering. In contrast to descriptive statements, prescriptive statements may be subject to negotiation or to searching for other alternatives.

2.3. Goals

2.3.1. *Nature and definition of goals*

Goals capture the different objectives that the system under consideration should achieve. The fact that this role has been acknowledged by researchers in requirements engineering has led to a new research avenue on the modeling and specification of goals, and a reasoning based on these to be adopted. This research, directed toward different applications, such as requirements development and verification or conflict management, assumes many forms: informal, qualitative and formal.

Zave and Jackson define a goal as an objective that the system under consideration must achieve. Goal formulations then refer to the properties that ought to be ensured via the system (Zave and Jackson 1997). These are optative statements, in contrast to indicative, and subject-delimited statements.

Typically, the system under consideration is analyzed within its organizational, operational and technical framework. Issues are reported and opportunities are identified. High-level goals are then identified and refined to address these issues and seize opportunities. The requirements are then developed to achieve these goals. This natural practice has led requirements documentation standards to include a specific document section dedicated to the goals that the system must achieve (ISO/IEC/IEEE 2018). More specifically, for automated information systems, goals can be used to link the future software to the management context (Yue 1993).

Van Lamsweerde (2001) states that goals:

– can be formulated at different abstraction levels, ranging from high-level strategic concerns to low-level technical concerns;

– cover different types of concerns: functional concerns associated with the services to be provided and non-functional concerns associated with the quality of service, such as safety, security, accuracy, performance, etc.;

– refer to the current or future system. High-level goals often refer to both systems.

According to Fickas and Helm (1992), the future system is essentially composite. It comprises both the software and its environment. It is made up of active agents such as people, devices and software. Contrary to passive agents, active agents have a choice of behavior. Unlike requirements, a goal may generally require the cooperation of a hybrid combination of several agents to achieve it (Dardenne et al. 1993). A goal under the responsibility of a single agent in future software becomes a requirement, whereas a goal under the responsibility of a single agent in the environment of the future software becomes an assumption. Unlike requirements, assumptions cannot be imposed by the future software. They will normally be satisfied by way of standards, regulations and legislation.

2.3.2. *Benefits of goals*

Goals have many advantages for requirements. They make it possible to:

– Verify the completeness of a requirements specification. It can actually be said that this specification is complete in relation to the goals if it can be proven that they are properly accounted for by the requirements described therein (Yue 1987).

– Verify the adequacy of the requirements. It can be said that a requirement is relevant to goals if its specification is used in the proof of at least one goal (Yue 1987).

– Explain and justify the requirements to the various stakeholders, in a similar way to design goals in the design process. A goal-refinement tree provides traceability links from high-level strategic goals to low-level technical requirements (Lee 1991).

– Structure complex requirements documents for increased readability. This is made possible because of their tree-like structure, which constitutes a natural structuring mechanism (Van Lamsweerde 2001).

– Investigate the many alternatives to consider during the requirements development process. Experience shows that refining alternative goals provides the right level of abstraction which decision-makers can be exposed to in order to validate the choices made or to suggest further alternatives that were previously overlooked. The refinement of alternative goals is a means of exploring proposals for alternative systems (Van Lamsweerde 2001).

– Manage conflicts between several points of view. Goals have been recognized to provide the roots for detecting conflicts between requirements and possibly resolving them (Van Lamsweerde 2001).

– Separate stable information from more volatile information for the management of changes in requirements. In fact, a requirement represents a particular way of achieving a specific goal. The requirement is therefore more likely to develop into another way of achieving the same goal than the goal itself. The higher a goal, the more stable it will be. The current system and the future system actually correspond to alternative refinements of common goals in the goals refinement graph, and therefore they can be integrated into a single goal model (Van Lamsweerde 2001).

– Identify the requirements that support them. Goals, together with scenarios, can be seen as essential tools that drive the systematic process of developing requirements (Van Lamsweerde 2001).

2.3.3. *Sources of goals*

Sometimes, goals are explicitly stated by stakeholders or in preliminary documents available to requirements engineers. However, goals are often implicit, such that their elicitation has to be triggered. Goals can be derived from several sources:

– The preliminary analysis of the current system allows the goals to be systematically identified. Such an analysis usually results in a list of problems and limitations that can be accurately formulated. This list of problems needs to be challenged in order to obtain an initial list of goals to be achieved by the future system (Van Lamsweerde 2001).

– The refinement and abstraction of a preliminary set of goals and requirements, already validated with the stakeholders, make it possible to derive many other goals. The point is to respectively ask "how" and "why" questions about the goals and requirements already available (Van Lamsweerde 2001).

– The resolution of conflicts between goals or obstacles to achieving goals results in identifying other goals. More sophisticated techniques have to be used for refining and abstracting goals, in particular through the use of scenarios (Van Lamsweerde 2001).

3

Existing Scales of Requirements

The purpose of this chapter is to present a literature review on the most common scales of levels of requirements. Two levels are possible with the first scale: "user" and "system". Two levels are possible with the second scale: "system" and "software". Finally, four levels of requirements are possible with the third scale, namely, "goal", "domain", "product" and "design".

3.1. "User–system" scale

The purpose of this section is to understand the two levels of requirements: "user" and "system" (Somerville 2016).

3.1.1. *User requirements*

The expression "user requirement" is used to designate any abstract (raw) high-level requirement of what the software system should do. This is a statement, in natural language in addition to diagrams, of the services that the system is supposed to provide to its users, and the constraints under which it must operate.

EXAMPLE 3.1.– *The e-lib software must generate monthly sales reports by book category such as kids', comedy and science fiction books.*

3.1.2. *System requirements*

The term "system requirement" is used to designate any detailed, elaborate, low-level requirement of what the system must do. It is a more detailed declaration, in formal or semi-formal language, of the functions, services and operational constraints of the software system.

EXAMPLE 3.2.– *When books are sold both as e-books and as hardcopy, then separate sales reports must be generated for each of the two categories according to a specific template.*

3.2. "System–software scale"

The purpose of this section is to understand the two levels of requirements: "system" and "software" (Van Lamsweerde 2009). The term "system" is used here to refer to the overall system, of which the software represents one of its components, such as an automatic braking system in an intelligent car, or an autopilot system in a modern aircraft. However, in the previous section, this term is used to refer to the software itself.

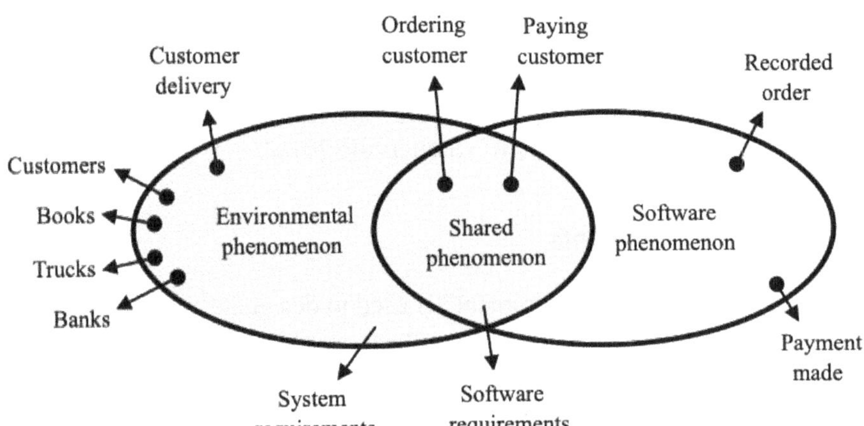

Figure 3.1. *Phenomena of the future software, its environment and requirements (adapted from Van Lamsweerde (2009))*

Van Lamsweerde considers that the requirements engineering process implies statements about the future system that differ in scope. In Figure 3.1, Van Lamsweerde explains how some statements can refer to phenomena belonging to the environment, without necessarily being shared with future software. On the other hand, other statements may refer to phenomena shared between the environment and the future software, that is, controlled by the software and observed by the environment, or vice versa.

3.2.1. *System requirements*

Van Lamsweerde uses the expression "system requirement" to refer to any prescriptive statement to be applied by the future software, as a component of the system, possibly in cooperation with other components of the system, and which must be formulated in terms of environmental phenomena.

System requirements must be understood and accepted by all stakeholders. This is possible due to their formulation in terms of the terminology used by these parts.

EXAMPLE 3.3.– *The sales system (the e-lib software, as well as other components such as stocks and delivery means) must allow bookshops to stock up on books under the best conditions.*

3.2.2. *Software requirements*

Van Lamsweerde uses the expression "requirement software" to refer to any prescriptive statement to be applied only by the future software, and which must be formulated only in terms of phenomena shared between the software and the environment.

Software requirements need to be understood and employed by developers. This is possible due to their formulation in terms of the software input/output variables in the terminology used by these developers.

This level of requirements corresponds to the two levels of requirements "user" and "system", as seen in section 3.1, but to two different levels of abstraction.

EXAMPLE 3.4.–

1) The e-lib software must generate monthly sales reports by book category (kids' books, fiction books, comedy books, science fiction books, novels, etc.).

2) If books are sold both as e-books and as hardcopy, then separate sales reports must be generated for each of the two categories according to a specific template.

3.2.3. *Relationships between system requirements and software requirements*

Van Lamsweerde uses the "four-variable model" to identify the relationships between the requirements of the two "system" and "software" levels as follows.

This model (see Figure 3.2) includes the following four types of variables:

– The monitored variables are environmental phenomena, which the software monitors by way of input devices such as sensors.

– The controlled variables are environmental phenomena, which the software controls by way of output devices such as actuators.

– Input variables are data that the software receives as input.

– Output variables are data that the software produces as output.

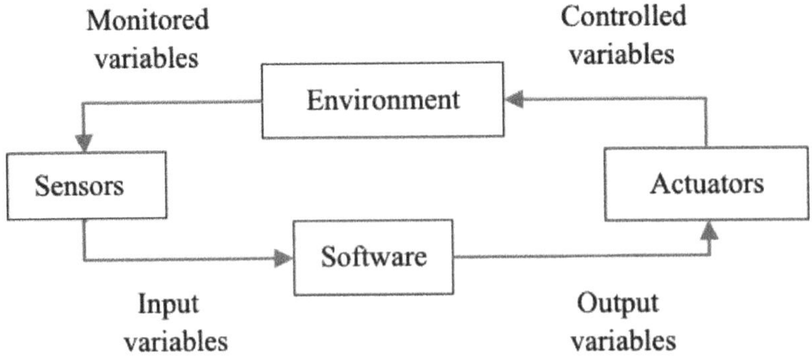

Figure 3.2. *Four-variable model (adapted from Van Lamsweerde (2009))*

As can be seen in Figure 3.2, input/output devices represent special interface components between the control software and its environment.

3.3. "Goal–design" scale

The purpose of this section is to understand the four levels of requirements: "goal"; "domain"; "product" and "design" of the "goal–design" scale (Lauesen 2002).

3.3.1. *Goal-level requirements*

These requirements express why the customer wants to spend money to acquire the product.

EXAMPLE 3.5.– *The e-lib software should increase the turnover of the "mylib" distributor by 5%, relative to book sales.*

3.3.2. *Domain-level requirements*

These requirements express the support of user tasks.

EXAMPLE 3.6.– *The e-lib software must facilitate the payment operation for booksellers by offering different payment channels.*

3.3.3. *Product-level requirements*

These requirements express a function to be provided by the future product. This level of requirements corresponds, on the one hand, to the two levels of requirements, "user" and "system", seen in section 3.1, but to two different abstraction levels, and, on the other hand, to the "software" level as seen in section 3.2.2.

EXAMPLE 3.7.– *The e-lib software must generate monthly sales reports by book category (kids' books, fiction books, comedy books, science fiction books, novels, etc.).*

3.3.4. *Design-level requirements*

These requirements express the interface details of the future product.

EXAMPLE 3.8.– *The e-lib software must provide the attached screenshots.*

Traditionally, a requirement must specify what the system should do without specifying how. If we specify "how", it initiates the design phase and it is then possible that alternatives that are better than those initially devised are excluded. In reality, the distinction between the "what" and the "how" is not clear. The right choice depends on the specific situation.

3.4. Discussion

In this section, we discuss the scales presented earlier.

In the "user–system" scale, a first-level requirement, "user requirement", designates any high-level abstract (raw) requirement of what the system must do. On the other hand, a second-level requirement, "system requirement", designates any detailed, low-level requirement of what the system must do. A certain inconsistency should be observed in this first scale. The first level is actually based on the notion of "user" role, while the second is based on the notion of system.

Moreover, in the "goal–design" scale, the design level is not a level as such. It is a particular form of the product level that focuses on the user interface aspect.

4

Existing Taxonomies of Requirements

The purpose of this chapter is to present a literature review on requirements taxonomies, focusing mainly on the five most common ones. The first taxonomy, RPAD, concerns the four categories: "requirements", "domain properties", "assumptions" and "definitions". The second taxonomy, KRSR, concerns the four facets of the requirements: "kind", "representation", "satisfaction" and "role". The third taxonomy, BNB, concerns behaviorist dichotomies. The fourth taxonomy, FS, proposes a systematic classification of the elements of requirements, such as components, objectives and constraints. Finally, the fifth taxonomy, FNF, concerns both the "functional" and "non-functional" types.

Van Lamsweerde (2009) states that the different taxonomy requirements offer many advantages in requirements management and engineering:

– The requirements categories make it possible to characterize more explicitly what they refer to, beyond their general definition, as normative statements to be applied by the future software.

– The requirements categories make it possible to characterize them more semantically in terms of prescribed behavior:

- Some requirements prescribe the desired behaviors.

- Some requirements exclude the unacceptable behaviors.

- Some requirements indicate the preferred behaviors.

– The requirements categories make it possible to differentiate between confined and transversal concerns:

- Functional requirements tend to relate to unique functionality features.

- Non-functional requirements tend to address cross-cutting concerns. The same requirement can restrict several units of functionality.

– The requirements categories enable useful heuristics to be produced for requirements:

- Some heuristics can help identify requirements that have been neglected.

- Some heuristics can help uncover conflicts between instances of requirement classes that are known to be potentially conflicting.

4.1. "Requirement–domain property–assumption–definition" taxonomy

The RPAD taxonomy distinguishes between four types of statements: requirement, domain property, assumption and definition (Van Lamsweerde 2009).

4.1.1. *Requirement*

A requirement is a prescriptive statement to be applied by the future software, possibly in cooperation with other components of the system. It is formulated in terms of environmental phenomena or only in terms of phenomena shared between the software and the environment.

The requirements refer to goals assigned to individual system agents.

EXAMPLE 4.1.– *The e-lib software must generate monthly sales reports by book category (kids' books, fiction books, comedy books, science fiction books, novels, etc.).*

4.1.2. *Domain property*

A domain property is a descriptive statement about the universe of the problem. It is supposed to hold invariably, regardless of how the system behaves, whether or not there is future software. Domain properties usually correspond to physical laws that cannot be broken.

EXAMPLE 4.2.– *A book (title) cannot appear multiple times in the same book order.*

4.1.3. *Assumption*

An assumption is a statement to be satisfied by the environment and formulated in terms of environmental phenomena. Assumptions are usually prescriptive, as they constrain the behavior of specific environmental components.

Unlike requirements, assumptions cannot be applied by the future software; they will be satisfied through standards and organizational regulations, physical laws, etc.

Assumptions refer to goals assigned to individual agents in the system environment.

EXAMPLE 4.3.– *A bookseller can only pay for a book order once it has been confirmed.*

4.1.4. *Definition*

Definitions enable domain concepts and auxiliary terms to be given an accurate, comprehensive and agreed meaning. Unlike statements of other types, definitions hold no truth value. It makes no sense to say that a definition is satisfied or not. However, the accuracy, completeness and adequacy of the definitions will need to be verified.

EXAMPLE 4.4.– *A customer of the "mylib" distributor refers to any bookseller who has a trade register authorizing them to carry out this activity.*

4.2. "Faceted" taxonomy

The KRSR taxonomy concerns a categorization of requirements according to four different criteria: "kind", "representation", "satisfaction", and "role". According thereto, the categorization to be chosen depends on the objective of the categorization (Glinz 2005):

– If the objective is general, its categorization is based on the "kind" criterion in order to differentiate, for example, a function requirement from a performance requirement. Table 4.1 summarizes the categories of the "kind" criterion.

– If the objective is to represent requirements, its categorization is then based on the "representation" criterion in order to differentiate, for example, an operational requirement from a quantitative one. Table 4.2 summarizes the categories of the "representation" criterion.

– If the objective is to verify the requirements, its categorization is then based on the "satisfaction" criterion in order to differentiate, for example, a soft requirement from a hard one. Table 4.3 summarizes the two categories of the "satisfaction" criterion.

– If the objective is to assign a role to requirements, its categorization is then based on the "role" criterion in order to differentiate, for example, a prescriptive requirement from a normative or presumed "assumptive" requirement. Table 4.4 summarizes the categories of the "role" criterion.

Nature	Definition
Function	A function that a system must fulfill.
Data	A data element or data structure that must be part of the system state.
Performance	A requirement relative to time (points in time, reaction time and time intervals), speed, volume or throughput (volume per unit time).
Specific quality	Qualities concerning both the operation properties of the product (for instance, reliability and usability) and managing the product (for instance, maintainability or portability).
Constraint	A design decision or design constraint imposed by a stakeholder (namely, an element that is not under the control of the system designers).

Table 4.1. *Nature-based requirements categorization (adapted from Glinz (2005))*

Representation	Definition
Operational	Operations or data specification.
Quantitative	Measurable properties specification.
Qualitative	Goal specification.
Declarative	Description of a required characteristic.

Table 4.2. *Representation-based requirements categorization (adapted from Glinz (2005))*

Satisfaction	Definition
Discrete	A requirement is either fully satisfied or not satisfied.
Continuous	A requirement can be gradually satisfied, that is, the degree of satisfaction is measured on an ordinal scale, at least.

Table 4.3. *Satisfaction-based requirements categorization (adapted from Glinz (2005))*

Role	Definition
Prescriptive	Properties that only concern the future system.
Normative	Norms in the system environment that influence the design and implementation of the future system.
Assumptive	Behavior of the actors that the future system cannot control.

Table 4.4. *Role-based requirements categorization (adapted from Glinz (2005))*

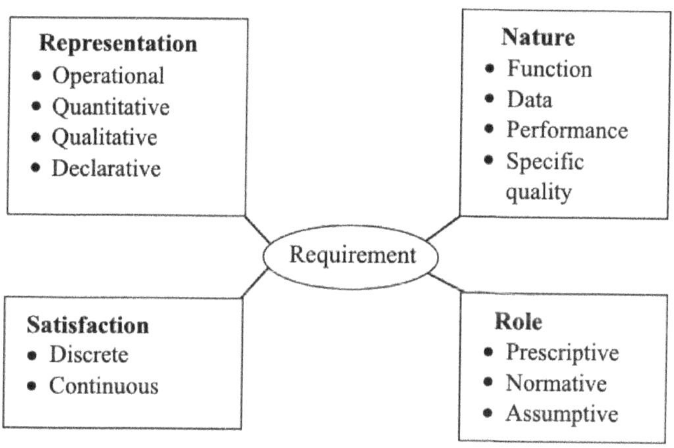

Figure 4.1. *Categorization of "faceted" requirements (adapted from Glinz (2005))*

Figure 4.1 summarizes the faceted categorization proposed by Glinz.

Table 4.5 applies "faceted" categorization to a given number of examples of software requirements.

Requirement statement	Requirement categorization
The e-lib software should calculate the total sales for each day.	Nature: function Representation: operational Satisfaction: discrete Role: prescriptive
The e-lib software must calculate the total amount including tax for a book invoice in accordance with the formula in use.	Nature: function Representation: operational Satisfaction: discrete Role: normative
The e-lib software must be easy to use by casual users.	Nature: specific quality Representation: qualitative Satisfaction: continuous Role: prescriptive
The response time of a search for a book in the e-lib software should be less than 1 s on average.	Nature: performance Representation: quantitative Satisfaction: continuous Role: prescriptive
The e-lib software must run on a PC with at least a 1,000 MHz processor and 1 GB of RAM.	Nature: constraint Representation: quantitative Satisfaction: continuous Role: prescriptive
The bookseller must provide accurate data in all input fields of the payment form in the e-lib software.	Nature: given Representation: declarative Satisfaction: discrete Role: assumptive

Table 4.5. *Examples of requirements with their categorization (adapted from Glinz (2005))*

4.3. "Behavioral requirements–non-behavioral requirements" (BNB) taxonomy

The BNB taxonomy concerns behavioral requirements versus non-behavioral requirements.

Broy (2018) bases the requirements categorization on a functional and architectural system modeling, including both logical and probabilistic behavioral models. In contrast to traditional categories, in which a distinction is made between "functional" and "non-functional" requirements, he suggests using the dichotomies of behavioral properties versus non-behavioral properties, to then structure behavior into logic versus probabilistic, and even further into black box behavioral views (interface) versus white box behavioral views. This results in an accurate and more consistent categorization of requirements.

4.4. "Fundamental categories–secondary categories" (FS) taxonomy

The FS taxonomy proposes, on the one hand, fundamental categories of requirements, which are separate from each other, and, on the other hand, secondary categories that form subcategories of the former (Meyer et al. 2019).

4.4.1. *Fundamental categories*

Every requirement defines a property of one of the fundamental categories described in Table 4.6.

Category	Definition
Component	The property according to which the system, project or environment includes a certain part.
Goal	A project or system objective, in terms of the desired effect on the environment.
Behavior	Property of the results or effects of the operation of the system or some of its components.
Task	The property whereby the project includes a certain activity.
Product	The property whereby a task uses or produces a virtual material or object.
Constraint	An environmental property that may affect components, objects, behaviors, tasks or products.
Role	A property whereby a component is fully or partially responsible for a behavior or task.
Limitation	The property whereby the project, system or environment does not include a requirement of any of the above types.
Lack	A property that should have a requirement, but that does not have one.
Meta-requirement	A property of the requirements themselves.

Table 4.6. *Fundamental categories of requirements (adapted from Meyer et al. (2019))*

4.4.2. *Secondary categories*

These categories, which represent particular cases of the previous fundamental categories, are described in Table 4.7.

Category	Definition
An actor	A human component.
A justification	A meta-requirement explaining the rationale behind a requirement (of any kind) in terms of objective.
A responsibility	A human role.
An obstacle	A goal defined as the need to overcome a negative property of the environment.
A functional behavior	Specifies the results or effects of the system.
A non-functional behavior	Specifies a property of how these results or effects are to be achieved.
A business rule	A constraint resulting from organizational practices.
A physical rule	A constraint resulting from the laws of nature.
An engineering decision	A constraint resulting from human choices.
An obligation	Describing a property that the environment is known to exhibit.
An assumption	Describing a property that the environment may or may not exhibit, but that the project may assume to hold for developing the system.
An invariant	Describing a property that is both an assumption and a behavior.

Table 4.7. *Secondary categories of requirements (adapted from Meyer et al. (2019))*

4.5. "Functional requirements–non-functional requirements" (FNF) taxonomy

The FNF taxonomy concerns functional versus non-functional requirements.

4.5.1. *Functional requirements*

According to Glinz (2007), the existing definitions of functional requirements follow two threads that largely coincide.

In the first thread, the focus is on functions: a functional requirement specifies "a function that a system [...] must be able to achieve" (IEEE 1990);

"what the system must do" (Somerville 2016); "a specification of what the system must do to satisfy the fundamental reasons for its existence" (Robertson and Robertson 2013). According to the latter, functional requirements should in principle be independent of any technology that will be used for implementing the system. The analyst is not trying to develop a technological solution, but rather to provide its functional specification. The specification of the "how" remains the responsibility of the designer. Lauesen (2002) defines functional requirements as a specification of system functions such as data storage, computation, transformation and transmission.

The second thread emphasizes behavior: behavioral requirements are those requirements that specify the system inputs (stimuli), the system outputs (responses) and the behavioral relationships between them, also known as functional or operational requirements (Davis 1993).

Wiegers, Jacobson, Rumbaugh, Booch and Somerville seek to provide a summary: "a statement of an element of required functionality, or a behavior that a system will exhibit under specific conditions" (Wiegers and Beatty 2013); "a requirement which specifies an action that a system must be able to perform, regardless of physical constraints; a requirement that specifies the input/output behavior of a system" (Jacobson et al. 1999); "statements of services that the system should provide, how the system should react to specific inputs, and how the system should behave in particular situations. In some cases, functional requirements may also explicitly state what the system should not do" (Somerville 2016).

EXAMPLE 4.5.– *The e-lib software must generate every day, for each catalog, a list of the books that are sold, with their quantities.*

Finally, Somerville considers that domain requirements are derived from the system application domain rather than from the specific needs of the system users. According to him, these may be new full-fledged functional requirements, constraints on existing functional requirements, or definitions of how particular calculations should be performed (Somerville 2016).

4.5.2. *Non-functional requirements*

Robertson et al. (2013) define non-functional requirements as properties or qualities that software must exhibit in order to be acceptable to its owner and operator. They propose eight categories of non-functional requirements.

– Look and feel requirements describe the intention of the appearance of the software. They are not a design of the interface. They include the following possible appearances: (1) simple, to be easy to use; (2) comply with the other software of the client; (3) attractive to children or another specific group; (4) innovative, appearing to be at the cutting edge of technology.

EXAMPLE 4.6.– *The e-lib software must have a simple and innovative user interface.*

– Usability requirements describe the compliance of the software with users in terms of experience and usage preference. They can be translated in terms of "easy to use" and "easy to learn".

EXAMPLE 4.7.– *The e-lib software must be usable by sales agents with limited experience in the use of computers.*

– Performance requirements describe the following aspects: speed to complete a task, results accuracy, operator safety, volume of data to be stored, allowed ranges of value, throughput such as transaction rate, efficiency in using resources, reliability, availability, fault tolerance and robustness, and scalability of the previous elements.

EXAMPLE 4.8.– *The e-lib software must ensure 10,000 simultaneous users in its "front-end" client part.*

– Operational and environmental requirements describe what the software must do to properly operate within its environment, when the software needs to collaborate with partner software or access external databases.

EXAMPLE 4.9.– *The e-lib software must collaborate with the banking software.*

– Maintainability and support requirements describe to what extent the software should be modifiable and what kind of support is needed.

EXAMPLE 4.10.– *The e-lib software has to be easily portable for other operating systems.*

– Security requirements are described in terms of three aspects, namely availability, confidentiality and integrity (Pfleeger and Pfleeger 2006) and a fourth aspect relating to auditing (Robertson and Robertson 2013).

EXAMPLE 4.11.– *The e-lib software must ensure that only authorized employees have access to the data.*

– Cultural requirements describe specific factors that could make the software unacceptable because of customs, religions, languages, taboos, prejudice or almost any other aspect of human behavior.

EXAMPLE 4.12.– *The e-lib software must offer a choice of the most common languages among customers.*

– Legal requirements describe software compliance with applicable laws.

EXAMPLE 4.13.– *The e-lib software must ensure the UNCITRAL Model Law on Electronic Commerce from 1996.*

In turn, Lauesen (2002) proposes the following categories of non-functional requirements:

– Data requirements specify what data the system should input, output or internally store; input/output formats; the communication state and the system state.

EXAMPLE 4.14.– *The e-lib software must store all the data of booksellers relating to their identities, orders, invoices and payments.*

– Quality requirements specify the extent to which the system must fulfill its functions. How quickly should it respond? How easy should it be to use? How secure should it be against attacks? How easy should it be to maintain?

EXAMPLE 4.15.– *The e-lib software should be easy to use by sales agents and should be organized in a way that minimizes errors.*

– The other deliverables include documentation, system installation, data conversion and user training

EXAMPLE 4.16.–

1) The e-lib software must be delivered with its technical documentation to facilitate its maintenance.

2) The e-lib software must be delivered after conversion of old data.

– Managerial requirements specify management aspects such as delivery times, price, legal responsibilities or intellectual property. The specification of the development process to be used can also be included. They are often considered as contractual issues.

Somerville defines non-functional requirements as constraints on the services or functions provided by the system. They include time constraints, constraints on the development process and constraints imposed by standards. Non-functional requirements often apply to the system as a whole, rather than to the individual functionalities or services of the system. In his opinion, these requirements, as their name suggests, are requirements that do not directly concern the specific services provided by the system to its users. They can be related to emerging system properties such as reliability, response time and storage occupancy. Alternatively, they can define constraints on the implementation of the system, such as the capabilities of I/O devices or the data representations used in interfaces with other systems (Somerville 2016).

Figure 4.2 shows a categorization of non-functional requirements, in which the three main categories are as follows: (1) product requirements that arise from the required characteristics of the software; (2) the organizational requirements originating from the organization developing the software and (3) the external requirements that originate from external sources (Somerville 2016).

– The product requirements specify or constrain the behavior of the software. They relate to performance requirements on the speed of execution of the system, and the amount of memory it requires, reliability requirements that define the acceptable failure rate, security requirements, usability requirements and dependability requirements.

EXAMPLE 4.17.–

1) The e-lib software must be available to all retail bookstores (7 days a week, 24 hours a day). The acceptable downtime should not exceed 5 minutes per day.

2) The e-lib software should be easy to use for sales agents and should be organized such that errors are minimized.

Sales agents must be able to use all the functions of the e-lib software after 6 hours of training. At the end of this training, the average number of errors made by experienced agents should not exceed half an error per hour of software use.

– Organizational requirements are general system requirements derived from the policies and procedures of the client's and the developer's organization. They concern the operational process requirements that define how the system will be used, the development process requirements that specify the programming language, the development environment or the process standards to be used, and the environmental requirements that specify the system operation environment.

EXAMPLE 4.18.– *Booksellers (customers of the e-lib software) must authenticate themselves using their trade register number.*

– External requirements include all requirements derived from external factors to the system and its development process. They concern the regulatory requirements that define what needs to be done in order for the system to be approved for operation by a regulator, such as a central bank, the legislative requirements that must be followed to ensure that the system operates within the law, as well as the ethical requirements that guarantee that the system will be acceptable to its users and the general public.

EXAMPLE 4.19.– *The software must apply customer privacy provisions, as indicated by the international business organizations.*

Glinz (2007) states that although the terminology "non-functional requirements" has been used for several decades, there is still no consensus on what they are and how they should be documented. He divides the issues in the "non-functional requirements" category into three types as follows:

– Definition issues: analysis of the existing definitions of these requirements shows both terminological and fundamental conceptual divergences. Different types of problems can emerge in these definitions: (1) lack of consensus on concepts; (2) ambiguity of some terms; (3) divergence in the scope of non-functional requirements; (4) explicit or implicit exclusion of project and process requirements.

– Categorization issues: analysis of the existing definitions of these requirements also shows quite divergent concepts for the categorization of non-functional requirements.

– Representation issues: the notion of non-functional requirement depends on the representation. A second representation problem is the lack of consensus on where to document non-functional requirements. For example, the two documentation models IEEE 830-1998 and Volere (Robertson and Robertson 2013) recommend that functional and non-functional requirements should be written in separate chapters.

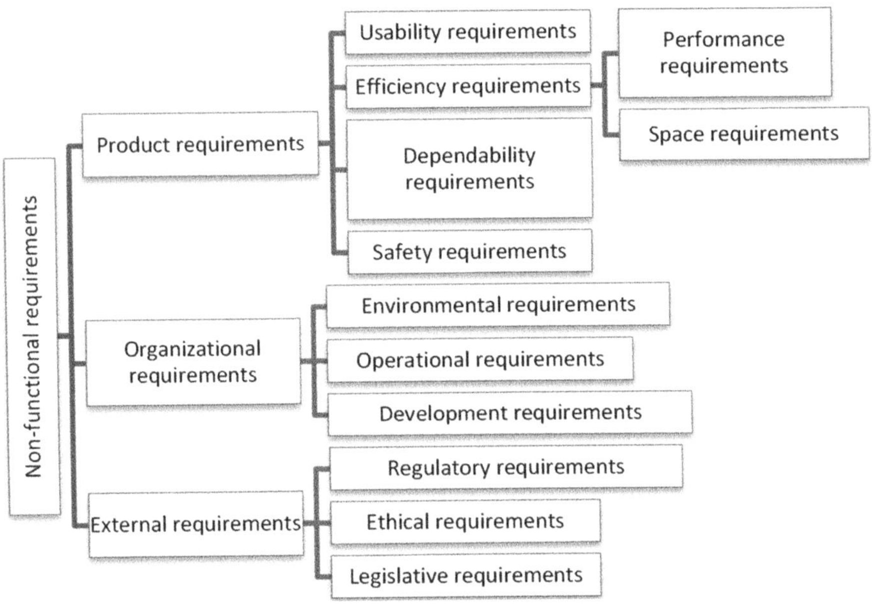

Figure 4.2. *Types of non-functional requirements (adapted from Somerville (2016))*

4.5.2.1. *Quality requirements*

Software quality is defined as a set of rules and principles to be followed during development in order to design a product that meets expectations (Abran et al. 2004).

The most well-known quality models today are hierarchical models that identify quality principles, starting from global requirements and the most general principles and moving down to the metrics that allow them to be measured (Mordal et al. 2011). Although there are many more or less standard quality models, it is not known which one to use. The answer is simple: none of them gives the whole truth, but they can be used as checklists. In some projects, a business standard must be followed, but even in these cases, other quality models must be consulted to identify important or risk areas (Lauesen 2002).

In this section, we present two standard models among the most common quality models.

4.5.2.1.1. The FCM model by McCall and Matsumoto

McCall and Matsumoto at the U.S. Air Force (McCall and Matsumoto 1980) proposed the FCM (Factors Criteria Metrics) model for evaluating software quality. The list of the 11 main factors, which represents an overall external view of quality, is presented as a two-level taxonomy. The top level distinguishes three major uses of the software: operation, review and transition.

– Operation: this is the daily use of the software by end users:

- integrity and security: to what extent the system handles physical disruptions and prevents malicious access attempts;

- correction: number of existing errors in the system;

- reliability: frequency of malfunctions of the system (MTBF, mean time between failures) and percentage of time during which it is available;

- usability: learnability of the system, efficiency in the execution of daily tasks, etc.;

- efficiency/performance: how quickly the system reacts, how many resources it uses, how accurately it computes values and so on.

– Review: this is software maintenance and extension:

- maintainability: how easily can errors be located and repaired;

- testability: how easy it is to test the system after a modification;

- flexibility: how easily can the system be expanded with new functionalities.

– Transition: this refers to running the software within a new technical environment:

- portability: how easily can the system be moved to a new software or hardware platform;

- interoperability: how easily can the system cooperate with other systems;

- reusability: how easy it is to reuse parts of the software in other systems.

These factors are characterized by 23 criteria that represent the internal vision of quality. Finally, the authors also proposed 300 metrics in order to measure these quality criteria. Flexibility, for example, could be measured as the average time necessary to extend the product with a new feature. The authors acknowledged, however, that such measures were unrealistic since it was impossible to define an average characteristic.

4.5.2.1.2. Standard SQuaRE or ISO/IEC model

Figure 4.3. *Organization of the SQuaRE series of standards (adapted from ISO/IEC 2006)*

The SQuaRE model comprises standards on software quality requirements and evaluation (Vaníček 2006; Castillo et al. 2010). The organization of these standards into divisions is illustrated in Figure 4.3 as follows:

– ISO/IEC 2500n – quality management division: in particular, ISO/document IEC 25 000, "Guide to SQuaRE", is the framework document for the SQuaRE series, which provides an overview and user guides thereof. It contains the SQuaRE architecture, terminology, intended users and associated parts of the series. It presents the entire SQuaRE series as a collection of quality engineering instruments.

– ISO/IEC 2501n – quality model division.

– ISO/IEC 2502n – quality measurement division.

– ISO/IEC 2503n – quality requirements division.

– ISO/IEC 2504n – quality evaluation division.

In this section, we only present the ISO/IEC 25010 (quality model) and ISO/IEC 25030 (quality requirements) divisions.

ISO/IEC 25010 standards

According to the ISO/IEC 25010 standard, a quality model is defined as a set of quality characteristics. Their relationships provide a framework for specifying quality requirements and for evaluating software quality, thus establishing a common understanding and terminology of software quality. The quality model also proposes three different visions of quality, namely, internal quality, external quality (see Figure 4.4) and operation quality (see Figure 4.5):

– The internal quality of the software provides a "white box" view and addresses the characteristics that are typically available during development.

– The external quality of the software provides a "black box" view and addresses the characteristics that are related to its execution.

– The software operation quality provides a "context" view and processes the characteristics that are related to its application context within its operational environment for the execution of user-specific tasks.

Internal quality has an impact on external quality, which in turn has an impact on the operation quality.

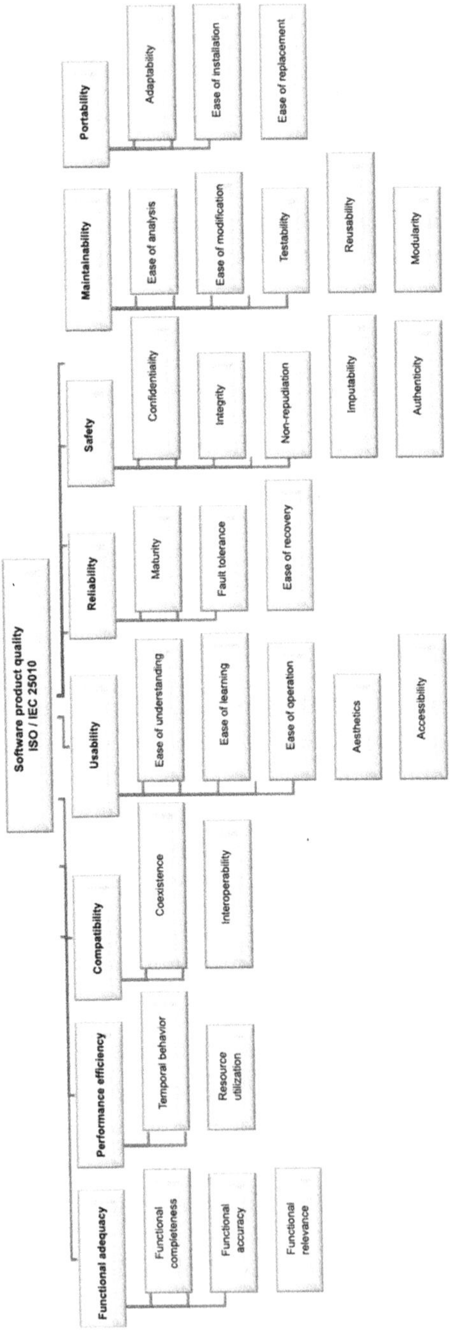

Figure 4.4. *Quality model for internal and external quality (adapted from ISO/IEC 25010 2007)*

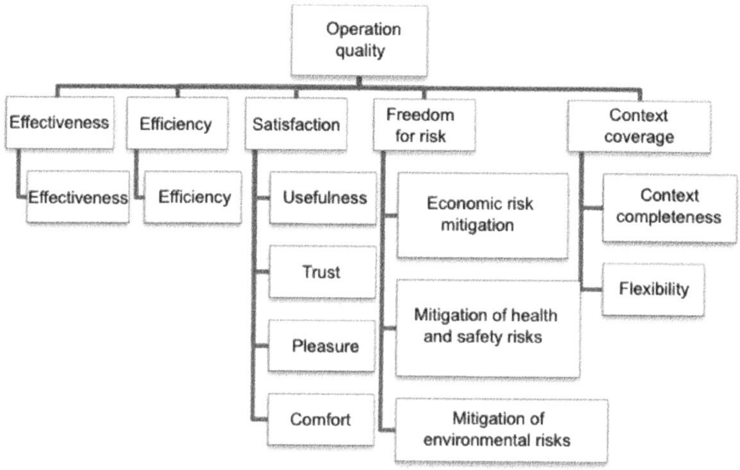

Figure 4.5. *Quality operation model (adapted from ISO/IEC 25010 2007)*

ISO/IEC 25030 standards

According to the recently adopted SQuaRE standard on quality requirements (ISO/IEC 2006), the software is usually integrated into a larger, more complex system. System and software requirements are closely linked, so they cannot be processed in silos.

It is therefore important to consider software quality requirements as a significant part of the software requirements specification at an early stage. The ISO/IEC 25030 standard considers software quality requirements from a system perspective. They are categorized according to the quality model of the ISO/IEC 25010 standard. The latter is a hierarchy of characteristics, sub-characteristics and attributes (measurable elements).

Attributes specify the software quality requirements in terms of measures and target values. The standard provides recommendations and guidance for specifying these requirements. It must ensure that they are clearly and precisely stated, in line with the needs of stakeholders, and that they are accurate, comprehensive, consistent, verifiable and measurable.

The ISO/IEC 25030 standard establishes a guide for identifying software quality requirements, validating the completeness of the requirements specification and identifying quality assurance and acceptance criteria for software.

System requirements are a precise formulation of the requirements of the stakeholders. They are considered to be the technical view of the requirements. They are verifiable and indicate the characteristics that the system must exhibit to satisfy the requirements of the stakeholders. System requirements may include requirements for software, computer equipment, data, the organization of human enterprise and may originate from various stakeholders, including end-users, organizations and official bodies.

The ISO/IEC 25030 standard focuses primarily on software requirements. According to the categorization that it presents, the software requirements concern: (A) the software product or (B) the software development process. The software product requirements include (a) the functional requirements, (b) the quality (inherent property requirements) and (c) management requirements (assigned property requirements). The functional requirements include (1) application-specific requirements as well as (2) functional requirements of the user.

4.6. Other taxonomies

In this section, we present three other taxonomies of requirements that exist in the literature, which are less widespread than the previous ones.

4.6.1. *"Primary requirements–derived requirements" (PD) taxonomy*

The PD taxonomy concerns the primary requirements versus the derived requirements. The first category of requirements originates directly from the stakeholders. The second category of requirements is derived from the primary requirements. This relationship implies that an analysis has been performed and that the derived requirement represents a need that can meet the intent of the primary requirement.

A derived requirement is a requirement that is deduced or inferred from a set of requirements in a particular system. The higher level requirement is called the "parent requirement" while the requirement derived therefrom is called the "child requirement". A derived requirement is typically identified during the elicitation of the stakeholders' requirements, needs analysis, business studies or validation (ISO/IEC/IEEE 2018).

4.6.2. *"Business requirements–technical requirements" (BT) taxonomy*

The BT taxonomy is concerned with business requirements versus technical requirements. Concerning the business requirements, the first category describes what needs to be delivered or achieved to produce value, such as increasing profits or improving customer satisfaction. These requirements are usually written by someone who understands the business process. Not all of these requirements need to be translated into technical requirements, as they may not be satisfied. However, in any case, they provide an overall idea of what should be in terms of the business.

Concerning the technical requirements, the second category explains how the software is supposed to do it. It refers to requirements that have a technical basis, such as the need to support a particular platform or the request for a specific interface with other systems. These requirements describe how software should do something and are mainly a representation of how to achieve the given business requirements. Technical requirements must be written by a technician. These requirements mainly explain the architecture of the software and its interfaces with other systems and software.

The artificial separation between the two categories means that technicians are ignored in business questions, and managers are ignored in technical questions. Therefore, the main objective of jointly writing business and technical requirements is to help make an informed decision during software development (de Waal 2016).

4.6.3. *"Product requirements–process requirements" (P2) taxonomy*

The P2 taxonomy is concerned with product requirements versus process requirements. The first category, concerning product requirements, describes software at a high level. It meets business requirements and is usually formulated in terms of the functionalities that the system must achieve. The second category, concerning process requirements, describes "how". It prescribes the processes that must be followed and the constraints that have to be complied with in order to produce the software (Aurum et al. 2005).

4.7. Discussion

In this section, we discuss the taxonomies presented above by showing their limitations. We start with some taxonomies that present some ambiguity and inconsistency. For example, in the first categorization (FNF), only the first category "functional requirements" is more or less well defined, where the emphasis is placed on either (1) the function, "a function that a system [...] must be able to achieve" (IEEESTD 1990), "what the system must do" (Somerville 2016), "what the system must do to satisfy the fundamental reasons for its existence" (Robertson and Robertson 2013), "a system function such as the capture, the computation, the transformation and the transmission of data"; or on (2) the behavior "the system inputs (stimuli), the system outputs (responses) and the behavioral relationships between them" (Davis 1993). However, the second category, "non-functional requirements", is simply defined by the negation of the first, that is, everything that is not functional is part of it. This makes its heterogeneous content difficult to analyze and manage.

Moreover, other taxonomies, such as "KRSR", can prove overly complex and difficult to understand. They can include many categorization criteria and categories that are too specific, which can make them difficult for analysts to use. Others, such as "BT" and "P2", are too rigid and do not allow the requirements to be adapted to the specific needs of a given software development project. They may impose predefined categories that do not cover all real-world situations, limiting their usefulness. There may be redundancy and overlapping issues in some taxonomies such as "FNF", where some categories or sub-categories overlap or repeat themselves unnecessarily. This can make the organization and categorization of requirements confusing and can lead to duplication of effort.

There is no clear standard or consensus on how software requirements should be categorized. Consequently, different taxonomies may be used in different organizations or industries, making it difficult to compare or consolidate requirements across different projects. Existing taxonomies can be difficult to update or evolve over time. Technological changes, evolutions in software development practices and new methodologies can make some categorizations obsolete, thus the need for constant adaptation of taxonomies.

Eckhardt (2017) carried out a detailed analysis of how professionals categorize requirements, explaining the rationale and the impact on the overall development process, and then analyzing the relevance of a categorization based on a system model as well as the problems of categorizing requirements in practice. Finally, he presented an approach that integrates such a categorization of requirements into future development activities. Broy (2018) further states that the characterizations of these categories often remain vague, inaccurate, and lack semantic consistency and uniformity.

PART 2

SMART: A Systemic Approach to Categorizing and Modeling Requirements

5

Conceptualization

The aim of this chapter is to propose a new approach named SMART (Systemic Approach to caTegorizing and Modeling Requirements), which is based on a holistic view of requirements. It consists of conceptualizing the requirements by considering all the parameters involved in their delineation.

The conceptualization of this approach means here, first of all, the construction of a representation that should be abstract and comprehensive of the subjects covered by the requirements and the factors that influence them. Then, it involves proposing a definition for the requirements and a hybrid categorization that facilitates its operationalization.

5.1. A new reference framework

In this section, we propose the requirements reference framework named R2F for precisely defining all the elements related to the software and its two development and operation environments. It thus consists of a two-dimensional frame of reference: (1) the first dimension concerns the generic subjects of the requirements, namely, the software and its two development and operation environments, as well as their descendants; (2) the second dimension concerns generic requirements factors that cover the following two aspects: quality and compliance.

For a color version of all the figures in this chapter, see www.istc.co.uk/chikh/smart.zip.

Although R2F can be made generic enough to be able to support all requirements in general, in this book we consider its application to addressing requirements in the field of software engineering only. This framework will then be employed to propose a better definition of requirements and a hybrid categorization of requirements, which combines several taxonomies and scales.

5.1.1. *Dimension 1: requirements subjects*

This dimension concerns the generic subjects of the requirements, which designate the parts of the future software to be described by the requirements. It is structured in the form of a hierarchy of subjects. Here, we present the complete tree structure of this dimension, the first level of which consists of the following three main subjects (see Figure 5.1): (1) "software", (2) "operation environment" and (3) "development environment".

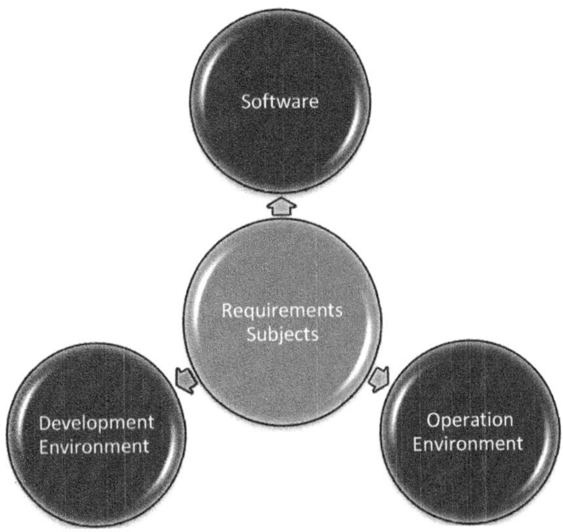

Figure 5.1. *Dimension 1: requirements subjects*

In order to make this dimension extensible, an "other subject" descendant is added to the second-level subjects: (1) "process support", (2) "human support", (3) "software support", (4) "hardware support" and (5) "cognitive context" of the two environments "operation environment" and "development environment". Analysts will be responsible for defining this new subject in order to adapt it to the context of their project. This new subject is not depicted in Figures 5.3 and 5.4 to avoid cluttering them.

5.1.1.1. *The software subject*

The "software" subject concerns the future software. In our case study, it corresponds to the "e-lib" software. This is mainly the software itself or possibly one of its following versions (possible extensions), for which the new requirements are to be described.

This subject includes the following four first-level descendants (see Figure 5.2):

– The "function" subject concerns the functionalities of the future software.

– The "data" subject concerns the data to be stored by the future software, all functionalities combined.

– The "user interface" subject concerns the user interfaces of the future software.

– The "technical interface" subject concerns the technical interfaces of the future software, with other software.

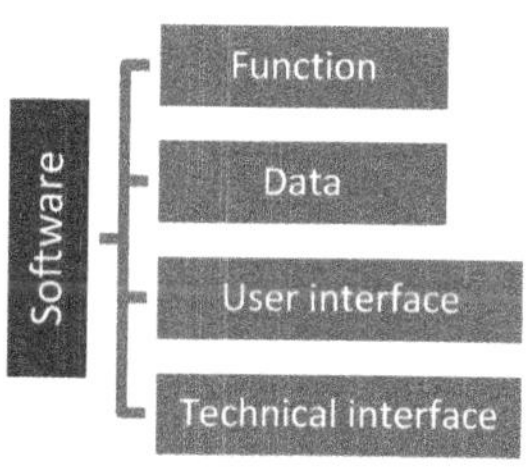

Figure 5.2. *Software subject*

5.1.1.2. *The software operation environment subject*

The "operation environment" subject concerns the usage environment of the future software. In our case study, it corresponds to the usage environment of the "e-lib" software. We present below the complete tree structure of this subject, the first level of which consists of the following five first-level descendants (see Figure 5.3): (1) "process support for operation", (2) "human support for operation", (3) "software support for operation",

(4) “hardware support for operation”, and (5) “cognitive context for operation”:

– The “process support for operation” subject, which concerns the procedural operation support, identifies the operation activities of the future software. It includes the following level 2 descendant: the “operation activity” subject; it covers the different operation activities of the future software. These are the operational or decision-making activities of the domain or the whole system that the future software must support, such as delivery or invoicing (information system); assist, such as medical diagnosis; maintain (business system); or control, such as the automatic braking mechanism in a car or autopilot in an airplane (embedded system).

– The “human support for operation” subject, which concerns the human operation support, identifies the end-users of the future software. It includes the following level 2 descendants:

- the “internal actor” subject, which concerns the company’s internal actors (employees) who directly use the future software in the context of their work;

- the “external actor” subject, which concerns actors outside the company, who interact directly with the future software, such as customers, suppliers and other partners;

- the technical assistance agents, who may be internal or external actors, may be responsible for the maintenance of the future software, unless the latter is fully autonomous.

– The “software support for operation” subject, which concerns the software operation support, identifies the new software platform of the future software. It includes the following level 2 descendants:

- the “operating system” subject, which concerns the operating system(s) under which the future software must be run;

- the “other software” subject, which concerns other local or online software or databases necessary for the operation of the future software in question, which can be coupled with it through the technical interfaces described in the “technical interface” subject from the “software” subject;

- the “existing data” subject, which concerns the existing data to be recovered from the existing software into the future software;

- the "social media" subject, which concerns the media that will be used to share the best practices and user experiences of the future software, such as a blog, wiki or focus groups;

- the "documentation" subject, which concerns the different types of documentation delivered with the future software, such as the user guide, technical documentation and marketing literature.

– The "hardware support for operation" subject, which concerns the hardware operation support, identifies the new hardware platform of the future software. It includes the following level 2 descendants:

- the "computer" subject, which concerns the computer and the server on which the future software will be installed. This includes a description of the elements such as the CPU required to run the future software; the storage unit such as disk and magnetic tape, required for storing the data of the future software; the various input/output units of the future software, such as the keyboard, mouse, scanner, player, audio/video recorder, screen, printer and touch screen, required for the exchange of data of the future software with the outside world;

- the "digital device" subject, which concerns other digital devices such as the sensor and the actuator, required by the future software;

- the "networking" subject, which concerns the equipment necessary for the computer network, such as the hub, switch, router, bridge, gateway, modem, repeater and access point, required by the future software.

– The "cognitive context for operation" subject, which concerns the cognitive operation context, identifies the concepts, goals and rules relating to the field of application of the future software. It includes the following level 2 descendants:

- the "concept" subject, which concerns the concepts underlying the field of application of the future software;

- the "goal" subject, which concerns the goals underlying the field of application of the future software as well as the business goals that the company is trying to achieve with the future software, which can be translated into tangible gains;

- the "rule" subject, which concerns the rules underlying the field of application of the future software, such as the physical or business rules, applied by the functions of the future software.

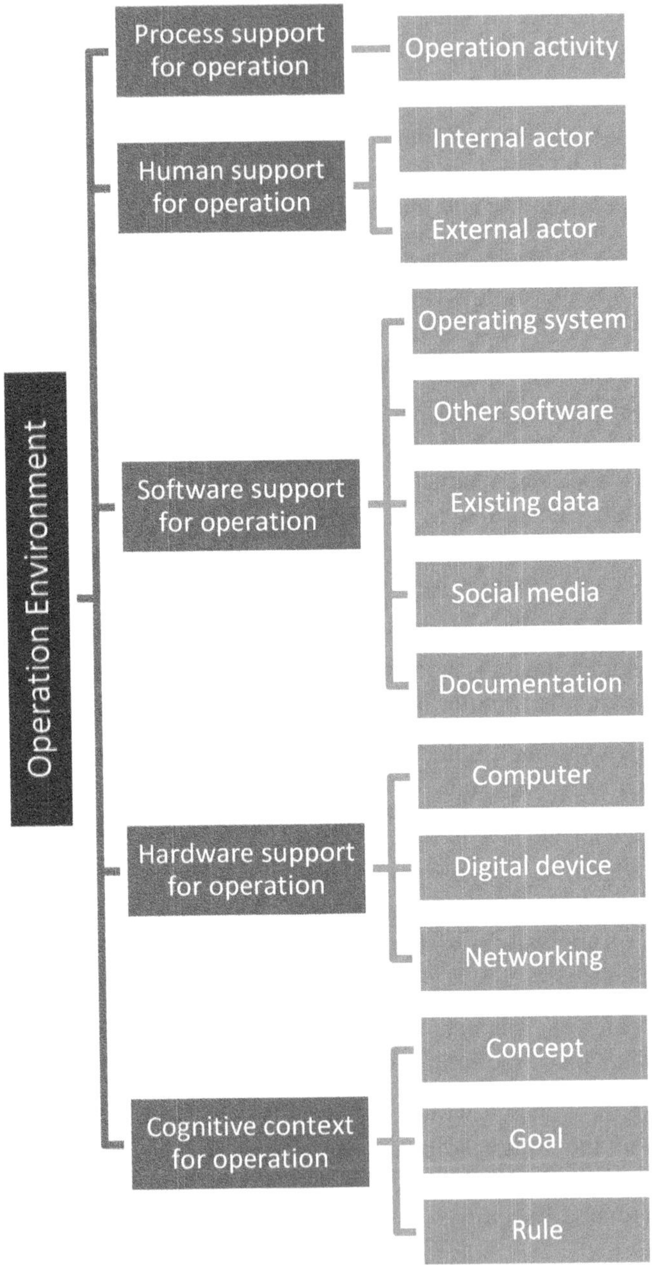

Figure 5.3. *Software operation environment subject*

5.1.1.3. *The software development environment subject*

The "development environment" subject concerns the development environment of the future software. In our case study, it corresponds to the development environment of the "e-lib" software. In the following, we present the whole tree structure of this subject, the first level of which consists of the five first-level descendants (see Figure 5.4): (1) "process support for development", (2) "human support for development", (3) "software support for development", (4) "hardware support for development" and (5) "cognitive context for development":

– The "process support for development" subject, which concerns the procedural development support, identifies the development activities of the future software. It includes the following level 2 descendant: the "development activity" subject, which concerns the various development activities of the future software such as the requirements analysis phase of the future software through the elicitation, analysis, specification and validation activities; the overall design phase, which concerns the construction of the architecture of the future software; the detailed design phase, which concerns the design of the various subjects of the future software, such as the database and the user interface; and the implementation phase, which concerns code production for the future software.

– The "human support for development" subject, which concerns the human development support, identifies the different categories of developers. It includes the following level 2 descendants:

- the "analyst" subject, which concerns the analysts who are involved in the analysis phase;

- the "designer" subject, which concerns the designers who are involved in the two phases of overall and detailed design;

- the "programmer" subject, which concerns programmers who are involved in the implementation phase;

- the "tester" subject, which concerns the testers who are involved in the test phase;

- the "other developer" subject, which concerns the other actors who are directly or indirectly involved in developing the future software.

– The "software support for development" subject, which concerns the software development support, identifies the software engineering workshop

(CASE tools), the integrated development environment (IDE), or any other software for the development of the future software. It includes the following level 2 descendants:

- the "CASE tools" subject, which concerns the software engineering workshop used in the development of the future software;

- the "IDE" subject, which concerns the IDE used in the development of the future software;

- the "library" subject, which concerns the libraries of reusable patterns or components, which must be combined with the first two subjects.

– The "hardware support for development" subject, which concerns the hardware development support, identifies the hardware platform for the development of the future software. It includes the following level 2 descendants:

- the "computer" subject, which concerns the computer and the server on which the future software must be developed. This involves describing elements such as the CPU to run the case tools and the IDE; the storage unit, such as disk and magnetic tape, required for storing the development artifacts of the future software (code, documents, diagrams and deliverables); and the various input/output units, such as keyboard, mouse, scanner, audio/video player and recorder, monitor, printer and touch screen, required for exchange with the outside world;

- the "digital device" subject, which concerns other digital devices, such as the sensor and actuator, required for the development of the future software;

- the "networking" subject, which concerns the hardware necessary for the computer network, such as the hub, switch, router, bridge, gateway, modem, repeater and access point, required for the development of the future software.

– The "cognitive context for development" subject, which concerns the cognitive development context, identifies the different methodological choices of the future software. It includes the following level 2 descendants:

- the "architecture" subject, which concerns the architecture to be used in development, such as the "3-tier" architecture;

- the "method" subject, which concerns the development method to be used, such as Merise, Remora and OMT;

- the "technique" subject, which concerns the development technique to be used, such as interview, observation and prototyping;

- the "artifact" subject, which concerns the different artifacts to be used that will be produced during development, such as a class diagram, business diagram, sequence diagram or test plan.

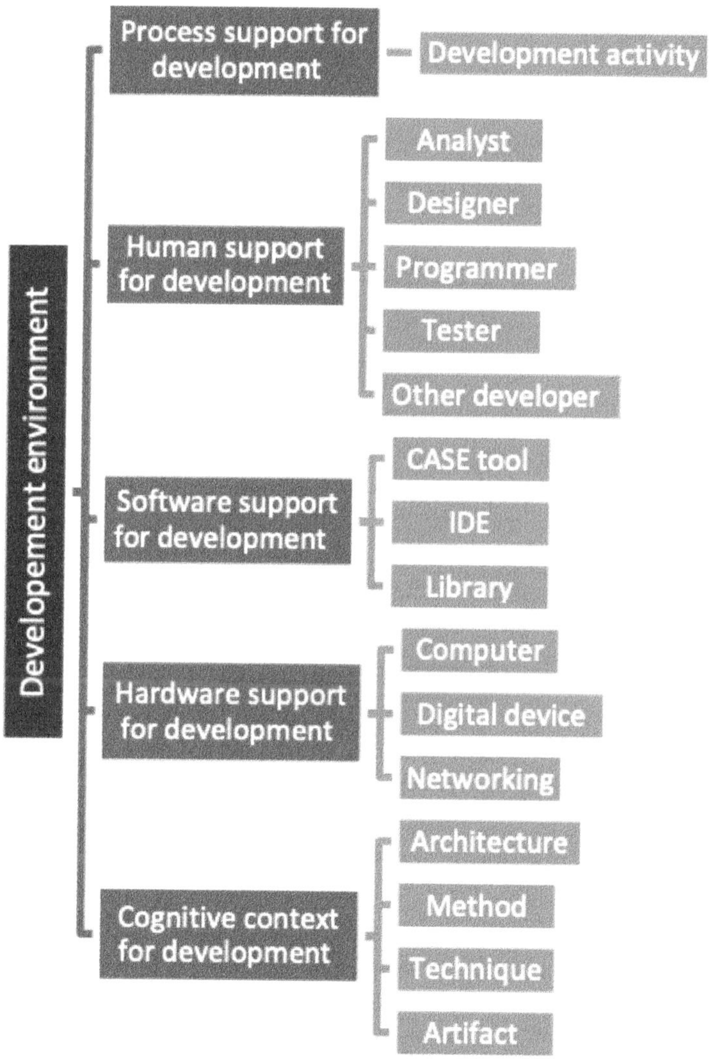

Figure 5.4. *Software development environment subject*

5.1.2. *Dimension 2: requirements factors*

This dimension concerns generic requirements factors. These are potential contingency factors that condition the requirements of the future software. It is structured as a hierarchy of factors. In the following, we present the whole tree structure of this dimension, the first level of which consists of the two main factors (see Figure 5.5): (1) "quality" and (2) "compliance".

These factors are alternately replaced in the literature by related expressions such as context, conditions, circumstances and constraints. In this book, we prefer the term "factors" to highlight their effects on the subjects.

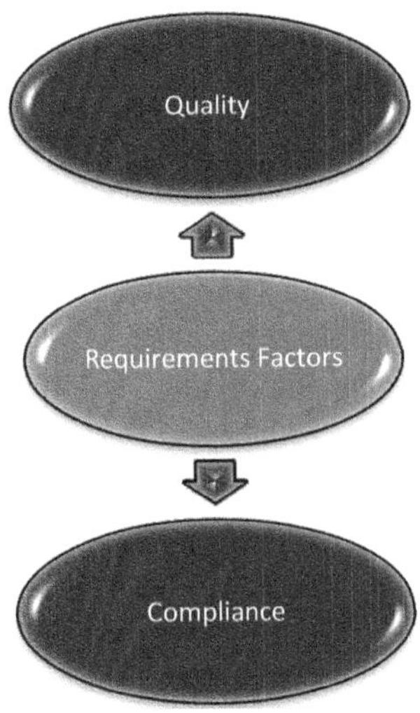

Figure 5.5. *Dimension 2: requirements factors*

5.1.2.1. *Quality factors*

These are the contingency factors, related to quality, which can affect the future software. We adopt the quality model of the ISO/IEC 25010 standard (see section 4.5.2.1.2), which includes the following factors (see Figure 5.6): "functional adequacy", "performance", "interoperability", "usability", "reliability", "security", "maintainability" and "portability".

This quality model comprises eight factors, broken down into sub-factors. It also allows the user to hierarchically derive other factors. It thus attempts to cover all the quality aspects of interest for most software.

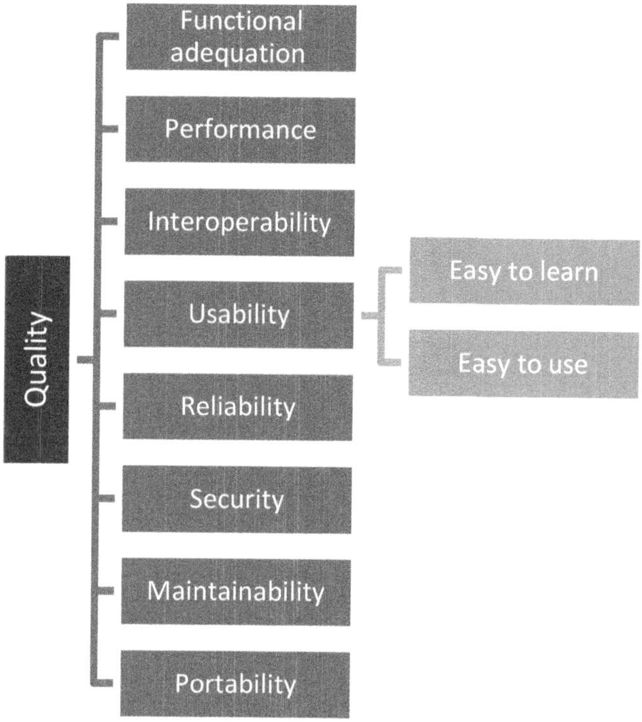

Figure 5.6. *Quality factors*

5.1.2.2. *Compliance factors*

These are the contingency factors, related to compliance, that can affect the future software. We propose a compliance model that includes the following seven factors (see Figure 5.7): "management", "technology", "economics", "culture", "social", "politics" and "law". Each of these factors can in turn be broken down into a set of sub-factors. This model is mainly inspired by the work on non-functional requirements, presented in section 4.5.2, proposed by Robertson and Robertson (2013) and to a lesser extent by Somerville (2016) and Lauesen (2002).

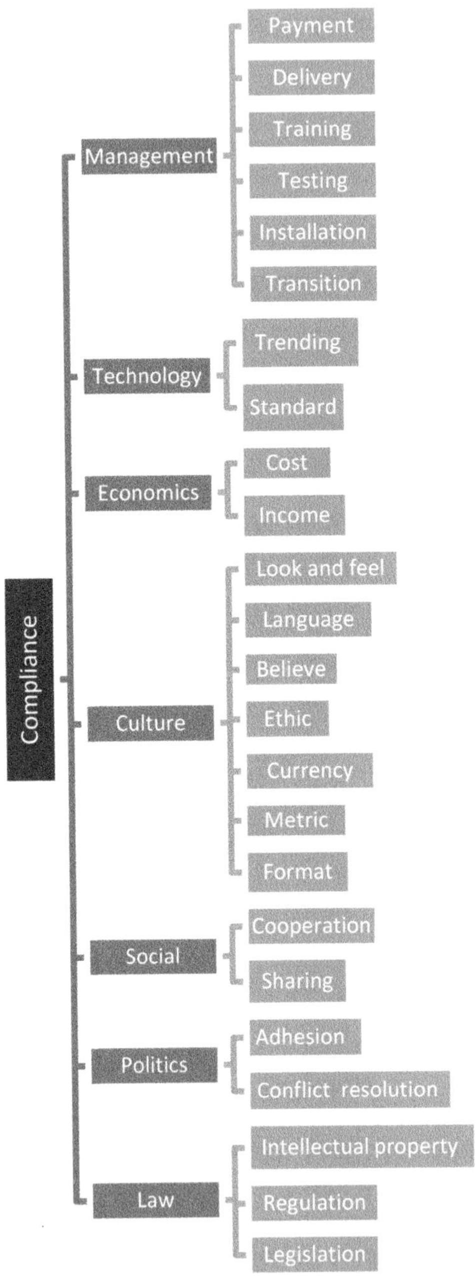

Figure 5.7. *Compliance factors*

In order to make this model extensible, a sub-factor "other" is added to the first-level factors. It will be the analysts' responsibility to define this new factor to adapt it to the context of their project. This factor is not shown in Figure 5.7 to avoid cluttering it.

5.2. New requirement definition

We use the elements (subjects and factors) of the R2F requirements framework, proposed in section 5.1, to define a requirement.

A requirement can be defined as an unambiguous and measurable statement, which can be:

– dependent on R2F: it corresponds to a statement structured according to a predefined model, expressed indirectly by users through the analysts. It represents:

- a need for operation or development service or support, associated with the generic requirement subjects of R2F,

- a quality property, associated with generic requirement subjects and the eight generic R2F quality factors,

- a compliance constraint, associated with generic requirement subjects and the seven generic R2F compliance factors;

– independent of R2F: it is an unstructured statement (free text), expressed directly by users or other stakeholders. It represents:

- a need for operation or development service or support,

- a quality property,

- a compliance constraint.

5.3. New scales and taxonomies of requirements

We use the elements (subjects and factors) of the R2F requirements framework, proposed in the previous section, to categorize the requirements, in particular the last taxonomy (E2) that is essentially based on this framework.

This section proposes two scales and two taxonomies for the categorization of requirements; it analyses their possible combinations and finally proposes a new hybrid requirements categorization approach based on a very specific combination.

5.3.1. *"User–analyst" (UA) requirements scale*

We propose a first scale of UA requirements (see Figure 5.8), composed of the two levels "user" and "analyst". It is based on the role of the author of the requirement, depending on whether they are the user or the analyst.

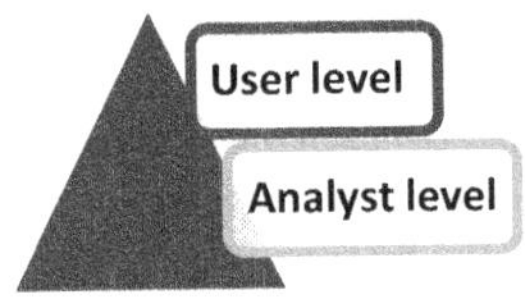

Figure 5.8. *"User–analyst" requirements scale*

5.3.1.1. *User level*

This level corresponds to the "user level" of the "user system" scale proposed by Somerville (2016), described in section 3.1.1. A requirement of the analyst level reflects the (high-level) superficial vision that the user has of the future software. It is informally (in natural language) and spontaneously expressed, directly by the user or another stakeholder. It corresponds to an unstructured (free text) statement. Hence, such a requirement does not usually comply with a predefined template.

5.3.1.2. *Analyst level*

This level corresponds to the "system level" of the "user system" scale, proposed by Somerville (2016), described in section 3.1.2. A requirement of the analyst level reflects the analyst's in-depth (low-level) vision of the future software. It is formally (mathematical expression) or semi-formally (mixed expression: textual and graphic) indirectly expressed by the user through the analyst, who acts on their behalf. It corresponds to a structured statement in accordance with a predefined template.

Several analyst-level requirements can be derived from a user-level requirement. In addition to knowledge of the field of application of the future software, the analysts responsible for deriving them must make efficient use of knowledge of the software market, which can be acquired either from commercial documentation or from market research.

In contrast to a user-level requirement, an analyst-level requirement must comply with a predefined generic structure, be validated by the various stakeholders, in particular the end users of the future software, and be testable, thus enabling that future software be tested against it.

In our course, we often use examples from outside the field of computer science to clearly explain the difference between a user requirement and an analyst requirement. We present two main examples, which relate to water consumption. The first example concerns a patient's need for drinking water, and the second concerns the need to fill an Olympic-size swimming pool with water for the purposes of high-level competition.

EXAMPLE 5.1.–

1) We consider the patient's need to drink (thirst) as a user requirement. It represents a natural need of this patient, which here refers to the user, without any details or technical specifications on the water. On the other hand, it is assumed that the response to this need (to hydrate the person) must involve an intermediate level, in which a doctor (who corresponds to the software analyst) must specify the optimal quantity to drink and the water quality (mineral and organic composition) that the patient requires, according to their state of health. We thus consider the doctor's latest specification as an analyst requirement.

2) We consider the need to fill the pool with water as a user requirement. It represents a natural need of the managers of this swimming pool, which here refer to the users, without any detail or technical specification of the water. On the other hand, it is assumed that the response to this need (filling the pool with water) must involve an intermediate level, in which experts (who correspond to analysts) must specify the water quality in terms of temperature, hardness, alkalinity and pH, chlorine and bromine levels or salt content according to the standards in this area. We therefore consider the experts' latest specification as an analyst requirement.

Finally, it is worth mentioning that the SMART approach will emphasize analyst-level requirements rather than user-level requirements.

5.3.2. *"Business–system–software" requirements scale*

We propose a second scale of BS2 requirements (see Figure 5.9), which is made up of the three levels: "business", "system" and "software". This scale corresponds to the first three levels of the Lauesen scale: "goal", "domain" and "product" from the "goal–design" scale (Lauesen 2002). We actually consider that the fourth level of the latter scale, which relates to "design", is simply a particular type of the "software" level, as we will explain below.

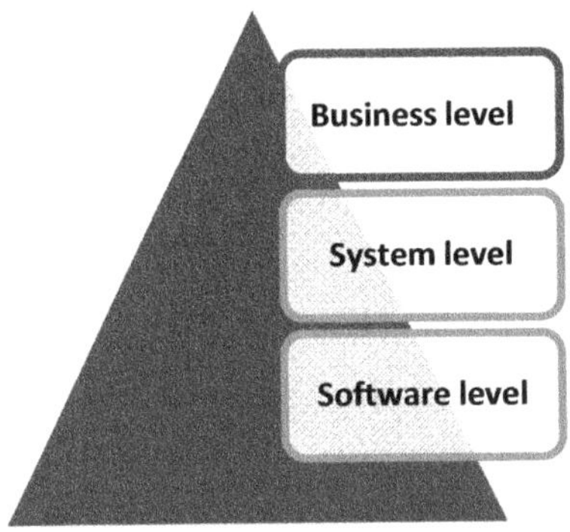

Figure 5.9. *"Business–system–software" requirements scale*

5.3.2.1. *Business level*

This corresponds to the "goal" level of the "goal–design" scale, which is described in section 3.3.1. Business-level requirements do not directly relate to the future software but rather to its usefulness to the owner company. The real requirements of the software will then be deduced by the designers as part of the solution.

First, the goals of the software must be identified in light of the limitations of the existing software and the opportunities to be exploited. This requires a thorough analysis of the goals, their ramifications and interactions. Finally, the point is mainly to link them with the strategic goals of the company listed in the "goal" subject. In fact, business-level requirements are the real requirements that the company seeks to satisfy. In fact, they are the only ones that will serve to justify the investment linked to the future software, in terms of added value. In some contexts, this added value is expressed in the form of financial gain to be provided, or financial loss to be avoided.

The responsibility for explicitly implementing these requirements in future software is thus left to the developers. They will be free to translate them into software-level requirements, as part of their design work. When software-level requirements are defined by the analysts as early as the analysis phase, they will invariably restrict the threshold of the solution proposed by the designers. In addition, the absence of the whole system and the field of application at this level further favors the designers by freeing them from a particular logic of operation.

However, there is a great risk for developers and analysts, who approve these requirements, of not being able to comply with them. This is because their satisfaction does not only depend on the software aspect of the solution, but rather on other aspects such as the skills of the users, market stability and the economic situation of the customer. A smart and diplomatic way to get around this problem is to use business-level requirements:

– at a specific location in the requirements document, such as the introduction or foreword, for the purpose of gaining the customer's trust, without any commitment from the authors to the customer. In fact, only the requirements contained in the named sections of this document formally represent the subject matter of the contract with the customer;

– as an introduction to the software-level requirements, which allows them to be contextualized and better documented by their direct association with business goals.

5.3.2.2. *System level*

This corresponds to the "domain level" of the "goal–design" scale, which is described in section 3.3.2. System-level requirements are not directly linked to the future software, but rather to its support of the system of which it is part. They specify the natural needs of the system without having to consider their implementation at the software level. The real requirements of the software will then be deduced by the designers as part of the solution. The system can here correspond to (1) a particular information system: human resources management and sales; (2) an embedded system for a smart car or a modern aircraft; and (3) a decision support system (DSS).

System-level requirements thus express decisional or operational activities of the whole domain or system that the future software must support, such as delivery or invoicing in an information system, decision-making in a DSS, or monitoring such as autopilot in an embedded system.

Among all the levels of the BS2 scale, the system-level requirements stand out for their realism and neutrality. In fact, by integrating them into the definition of the specifications, the customer avoids giving preference to a specific supplier or developer. This makes it possible, in a competitive situation, to offer equal opportunities to candidates for tender.

Furthermore, the formulation of the specifications by the analysts, at the system level, prevents them from interfering in design activities, thus leaving more freedom to the designers for proposing their solutions. Finally, this formulation will allow a natural structuring of the requirements based on the field of application. This will facilitate their identification and verification by analysts, and their understanding and validation by the various stakeholders.

The responsibility for explicitly implementing these requirements in future software is left to the developers. They will be free to translate them into software-level requirements, as part of their design work. In fact, when the requirements of the software level are defined by analysts in the analysis phase, they will indirectly limit the threshold of the solution proposed by the designers. However, the presence of the field of application makes the task of developers easier and more realistic than in the business level.

Finally, the analysts responsible for identifying these requirements must have sufficient knowledge of the system as a whole, which they can acquire either from the associated documentation or from the domain experts.

It should also be noted that the requirements of the system level are different from the system requirements. The latter, which fall outside the scope of our approach, concern the system itself, in which the software represents a subsystem. They are seen as part of requirements engineering, which is included in systems engineering. In contrast, system-level requirements are seen as part of software requirements engineering, which in turn is included in software engineering.

5.3.2.3. *Software level*

This corresponds to the “product level” of the “goal–design” scale, which is described in section 3.3.3. Software-level requirements relate directly to the future software. In contrast to system requirements, software requirements can be used maliciously by some customers to favor a particular vendor. Indeed, when defining the specifications, an unscrupulous customer can formulate software requirements that correspond to services exclusively offered by this supplier.

The formulation of the specifications, in terms of software requirements, subsequently affects the freedom of proposal among the designers, reducing their design potential.

Not relying on any domain or other logic, these requirements are often formulated by the customer by copying the characteristics of similar existing software. Consequently, some of them, which prove to be unjustified, redundant or even in conflict with others, become difficult to understand by the various stakeholders, be verified by analysts and be validated by the end users.

In order to compensate for these shortcomings, we propose to frame the software-level requirements with others among those from the other two levels “system” and “business”. In the first case, the software-level requirements need to be associated with the tasks of the domain that the software aims to support. In the second case, they have to be associated with the business goals that the software aims to satisfy. This will allow them to be put into their natural operation context.

However, as we pointed out at the beginning of section 5.3.2, we consider the “design” level of the “goal–design” scale as a particular type of the “software” level of our scale, in which the requirements are expressed in terms of “how”. But, unlike the Lauesen scale, which at this level merely considers user interfaces, we extend this particular type to the four subjects of the R2F frame of reference related to software, namely, “function”, “data”, “user interface” and “technical interface”.

We consider that software-level requirements become design requirements when they include choices of design-related elements, such as the screenshots for the "user interface" subject, the database schemes for the "data" subject, the algorithms for the "function" subject and finally the communication protocols for the "technical interface" subject.

Normally, software-level requirements should not interfere with design choices, clearly stating how to develop any software aspect. However, design requirements can be useful in certain situations, such as:

– subcontracting, in which a dialog is established between suppliers, in the event that the main software developer solicits several partners, and wishes to:

- ensure consistent support for the design of a particular aspect of the software, such as the database or human–machine interfaces. They can then resort to design requirements in order to enforce a specific design logic, otherwise the resulting deliverables will be very heterogeneous and difficult to integrate,

- maintain control over the design used by other subcontractors. They can then resort to design requirements in order to enforce a common design logic, otherwise it will not be possible to follow the specific logic of each of the partners;

– the future software belongs to a software family. The customer then wants the future software to be designed in a similar way to its predecessors in order to facilitate its integration into the family and to guarantee the end users the same working environment. In the latter case, the design requirements relate more specifically to user interfaces;

– reinforcement as examples of software-level requirements. Design requirements can be used as examples of solutions that can be inserted into the software-level requirements;

– design requirements can also be used in certain cases to impose user logic in the design of a particular software aspect, such as user interfaces. This last situation, which may be acceptable and logical in the case of tailor-made software, quickly becomes absurd in the case of a commercial-off-the-shelf (COTS) software. In this last example, imposing a specific interface is useless since the human–machine interface of the COTS software already exists and it is generally not an option to question it.

5.3.3. *"Endogenous–exogenous" requirements taxonomy*

We propose a new taxonomy for E2 requirements (see Figure 5.10), consisting of the two categories "endogenous requirements" versus "exogenous requirements". It is a generalization of the "functional requirements" versus "non-functional requirements" categorization (see section 4.5).

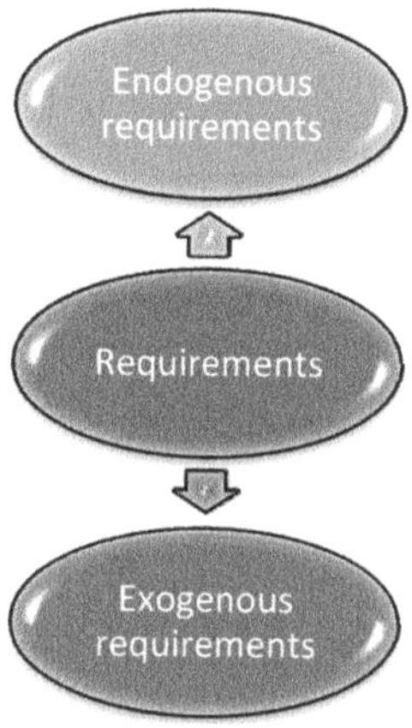

Figure 5.10. *"Endogenous–exogenous" requirements taxonomy*

An exogenous requirement can correspond to several endogenous requirements, while an endogenous requirement can correspond to several exogenous requirements.

5.3.3.1. *Endogenous category*

This consists of intrinsically describing a generic requirement subject (see section 5.1.1), identified from R2F (see section 5.1), by associating it with a specific subject suitable to the future software. The generic subject can be chosen from the R2F subjects, depending on the desired level of refinement, starting from the highest level, comprising three main subjects, to the lowest level, comprising atomic subjects.

This structural taxonomy of endogenous requirements (by requirement subject) is shown in Figure 5.11.

Endogenous requirements	**Software requirements**	Functional requirements
		Data requirements
		User interface requirements
		Technical interface requirements
	Operation requirements	Process support for operation requirements
		Human support for operation requirements
		Software support for operation requirements
		Hardware support for operation requirements
		Cognitive context for operation requirements
	Development requirements	Process support for development requirements
		Human support for development requirements
		Software support for development requirements
		Hardware support for development requirements
		Cognitive context for development requirements

Figure 5.11. *Structural categorization of endogenous requirements*

5.3.3.2. *Exogenous category*

This consists of extrinsically describing a generic requirement subject (see section 5.1.1), by applying a generic requirement factor (see section 5.1.2), identified from R2F (see section 5.1), by associating them with a specific subject and a specific factor of the future software. The generic subject can be chosen from the R2F subjects, according to the desired level of refinement, going from the highest level, composed of the three main subjects (1) "software", (2) "operation environment" and (3) "development environment", toward the lowest level, comprising atomic subjects. The generic factor can be chosen from the R2F factors, depending on the desired refinement level, from the highest level, comprising the two main factors (1) "quality" and (2) "compliance", toward the lowest level, comprising atomic factors.

Naturally, the whole set of categories of potential exogenous requirements cannot be obtained by a simple Cartesian product of the set of generic requirements subjects with the set of generic requirements factors. The reason is quite simple: many combinations are not applicable, either because they are of no interest, or because they are meaningless. Consequently, it would be preferable to build a matrix of valid exogenous requirement categories as a cross-referencing between subjects (in rows) and factors (in columns). The cells of this matrix, which correspond to an invalid cross, will be inhibited. Finally, we emphasize that valid categories of exogenous requirements do not present the same interest from the point of view of the importance of the subjects they cover, and the requirement factors they apply, on the one hand, and the specificity of the project under consideration, on the other hand.

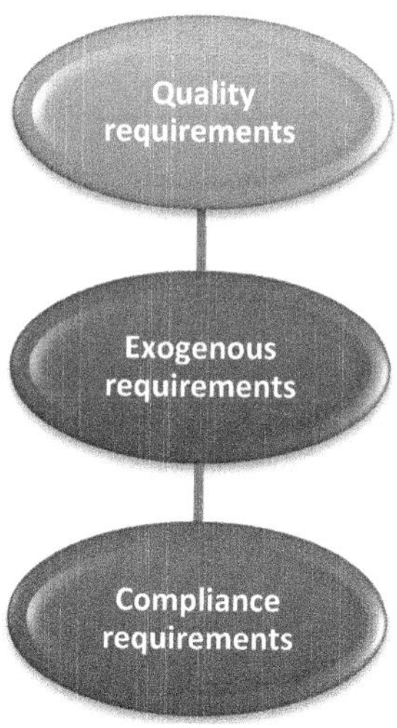

Figure 5.12. *Taxonomy of exogenous requirements by requirement factors category*

The new taxonomy of exogenous requirements is a generalization of that of the NFR category, which is very common in the software engineering literature (see section 4.5.2). In the SMART approach, the exogenous requirements, unlike non-functional requirements, are not limited to the quality aspects of the future software. On the one hand, they cover many other aspects that concern both the software itself and its two operation and development environments; on the other hand, they apply all the exogenous factors including both the quality of the software and its compliance with its interdisciplinary environment.

A taxonomy of exogenous requirements, by category of generic requirement factors, is shown in Figure 5.12.

5.3.3.2.1. Quality category

The "quality requirements" category is a subcategory of exogenous requirements, which is dedicated to covering the quality factors applicable to the four descendants of the "software" subject: "function", "data", "user interface" and "technical interface". The NFR category understood in the sense of quality and defined in the existing typology (see section 4.5.2) is a subcategory of exogenous requirements, dedicated to covering the quality factors applied only to the "function" descendant of the "software" subject.

Subjects	**Quality factors**							
	Functional adequation	**Performance**	**Interoperability**	**Usability**	**Reliability**	**Security**	**Maintainability**	**Portability**
Software	X	X	X	X	X	X	X	X
Function	X	X	X		X	X	X	X
Data		X	X		X	X	X	X
User interface		X	X	X	X	X	X	X
Technical interface		X	X		X	X	X	X

Table 5.1. *Matrix (quality factors–requirements subjects)*

5.3.3.2.2. Compliance category

The "compliance requirements" category is a subcategory of the exogenous requirements, which is dedicated to covering the compliance factors applicable to the three subjects – "software", "operation environment" and "development environment" – and to the descendants of their respective trees according to R2F (see section 5.1).

Subjects	Compliance factors						
	Management	**Technology**	**Economics**	**Culture**	**Social**	**Politics**	**Law**
Software	X	X	X	X	X	X	X
Function	X	X	X	X	X	X	X
Data	X	X	X	X	X	X	X
User interface	X	X	X	X	X	X	X
Technical interface	X	X	X	X	X	X	X
Operation environment	X	X	X	X	X	X	X
Process support for operation			X	X	X	X	X
Human support for operation	X		X	X	X	X	X
Software support for operation	X	X	X	X	X	X	X
Hardware support for operation	X	X	X	X	X	X	X
Cognitive context for operation							
Development environment	X	X	X	X	X	X	X
Process support for development			X	X	X	X	X
Human support for development	X		X	X	X	X	X
Software support for development	X	X	X	X	X	X	X
Hardware support for development	X	X	X	X	X	X	X
Cognitive context for development							

Table 5.2. *Matrix (compliance factors–requirements subjects)*

5.3.4. *Requirements taxonomy by nature*

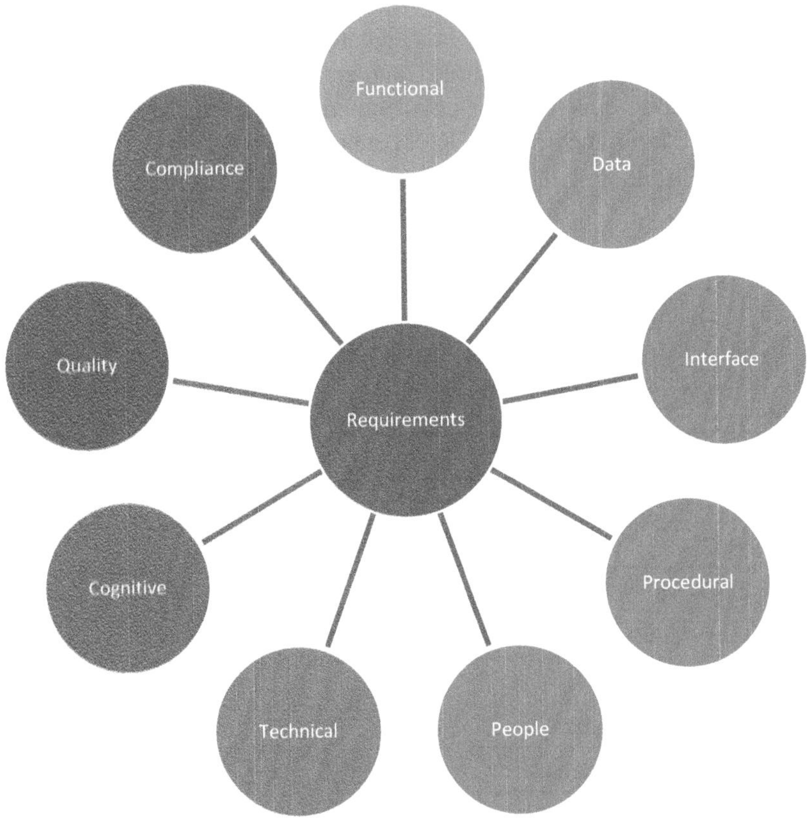

Figure 5.13. *Requirements taxonomy by nature*

This taxonomy of requirements is based on the nature of the generic subjects for endogenous requirements and the nature of the generic factors for exogenous requirements (see Figure 5.13). It includes nine categories:

– The "functional requirements" category concerns the functional endogenous requirements for specifying the functionalities of the future software. It corresponds to the "function" subject derived from the "software" subject of R2F.

– The "data requirements" category concerns endogenous data requirements for specifying the data to be stored by the future software. It corresponds to the "data" subject from the "software" subject of R2F.

– The "interface requirements" category concerns endogenous interface requirements for specifying the interfaces of the future software with its environment. It corresponds to the "user interface" and "technical interface" subjects derived from the "software" subject of R2F.

– The "procedural requirements" category concerns the process requirements for specifying the operation activities of the system as a whole that the future software must support, and the development activities of the future software. It corresponds to the "process support for operation" and "process support for development" subjects of the respective "operation environment" and "development environment" subjects of R2F.

– The "people requirements" category concerns the endogenous requirements of people for specifying the end users and the developers of the future software. It corresponds to the "human support for operation" and "human support for development" subjects of the respective "operation environment" and "development environment" subjects of R2F.

– The "technical requirements" category concerns the endogenous technical requirements for specifying the new software and hardware platforms of the future software as well as its software and hardware development environment. It corresponds to the "software support for operation" and "hardware support for operation" subjects derived from the "operation environment" subject, and to the "software support for development" and "hardware support for development" subjects from the "development environment" subject of R2F.

– The "cognitive requirements" category concerns the endogenous cognitive requirements of the two operation and development environments for specifying the operational context (concepts, goals and rules) for the former and the development context (methods, techniques, tools, models and tools) for the latter. It corresponds to the "cognitive context for operation" and "cognitive context for development" subjects of the respective "operation environment" and "development environment" subjects of R2F.

– The "quality requirements" category concerns the exogenous quality requirements.

– The "compliance requirements" category concerns the exogenous requirements relating to compliance.

The latter taxonomy generalizes Glinz's (2005) categorization, presented in section 4.2, which is based on the "kind" criterion.

5.4. New hybrid requirements categorization

In this section, we propose a new categorization of requirements. First, we explore the different possible cross-references of the three aforementioned categorizations, namely, the UA and BS2 scales, and the E2 taxonomy, in order to identify the appropriate combination.

The first cross-reference (see Table 5.3), which concerns the UA and BS2 scales, is of little interest. In fact, the E2 categorization, which constitutes the core of the SMART approach, is not taken into account. We note in this cross-reference that, on the one hand, users are more familiar with the requirements of the "business" and "system" levels than with those of the "software" level. Even more precisely, decision-making users are more comfortable expressing the "business" level requirements, and operator users are more comfortable expressing the requirements of the "system" level. On the other hand, analysts are more familiar with the requirements of the "software" level than with those of the "business" and "system" levels.

	Business	**System**	**Software**
User	Users (more familiar)	Users (more familiar)	Users (less familiar)
Analyst	Analysts (less familiar)	Analysts (less familiar)	Analysts (more familiar)

Table 5.3. *Cross-referencing of the UA scale with the BS2 scale*

The second cross-reference (see Table 5.4) concerns the UA scale and the E2 taxonomy. Unlike the previous one, this cross-reference refers to R2F through the E2 taxonomy. The two categories in the first column of the table, related to endogenous and exogenous requirements at the "user" level, can have several requirements subjects or factors at the same time. However, the other two categories in the second column of the table, related to endogenous and exogenous requirements at the "analyst level", can have only one requirement subject or factor at the same time.

	User	**Analyst**
Endogenous	Have multiple subjects at once	Have only one subject at once
Exogenous	Have multiple subjects and factors at once	Have only one subject and one factor at once

Table 5.4. *Cross-referencing of the UA scale with the E2 taxonomy*

The third cross-reference (see Table 5.5) concerns the BS2 scale and the E2 taxonomy. Like the previous one, this cross-reference refers to R2F through the E2 taxonomy. The requirements of the three categories in the first row of the table correspond to the "endogenous" type of the E2 taxonomy, all levels of the BS2 scale combined. The requirements of the three categories in the second row of the table correspond to the "exogenous" type of the E2 taxonomy, all levels of the BS2 scale combined.

We observe that in the two categories resulting from this last cross-reference, related to the exogenous requirements of the "business" and "system" levels, the specific requirement factor (SF) is unknown. It is therefore left to the designers, who are free to specify it in order to satisfy the specific business goal or to support the specific operation activity (SS).

Moreover, we also note that in the two categories resulting from this last cross-reference, related to the endogenous requirements of the "business" and "system" levels, the real requirement subject, related to the software and its operation and development environments (SS), is unknown. It is left to the designers, who are free to specify it in order to satisfy the specific business goal or to support the specific operation activity.

We propose a predefined template for each requirement category, resulting from cross-referencing the BS2 scale with the E2 taxonomy.

	Business	**System**	**Software**
Endogenous	The analyst defines the specific business goal the software should satisfy and specifies the GS, whose corresponding SS will be clarified later by developers.	The analyst defines the specific operation activity the software should support and specifies the GS, whose corresponding SS will be clarified later by developers.	The analyst defines the GS as well as the corresponding SS that the software should take in charge.
Exogenous	The analyst defines the specific business goal the software should satisfy and specifies the GF, whose corresponding SF will be clarified later by developers.	The analyst defines the specific operation activity the software should support and specifies the GF, whose corresponding SF will be clarified later by developers.	The analyst defines the GS as well as the corresponding SS and specifies the GF as well as the corresponding SF that the software should take in charge.

Table 5.5. *Cross-referencing of the BS2 scale with the E2 taxonomy. GS: generic subject; SS: specific subject; GF: generic factor; SF: specific factor*

Finally, our new hybrid categorization approach combines the UA and BS2 scales and the E2 taxonomy as follows:

– First, the requirements are categorized according to the UA scale. Next, the requirements in each "user requirements" and "analyst requirements" category are categorized according to the BS2 scale.

– Second, the requirements of each of the six categories of requirements, resulting from the previous classification, are classified according to the E2 taxonomy.

– Third, the requirements of each category of the 12 main categories of requirements, resulting from the previous classification, are classified according to a specific categorization of this category.

Table 5.6 presents all the possible specific categories proposed by the new hybrid categorization approach of requirements.

UA	BS2	E2	Specific categorization
User req.			User req. are unstructured req. which in practice do not refer to R2F
	A	1	User, endogenous, software level req.
		2	User, exogenous, software level req.
	B	1	User, endogenous, system level req.
		2	User, exogenous, system level req.
	C	1	User, endogenous, business level req.
		2	User, exogenous, business level req.
Analyst req.			Analyst requirements are structured req. which refer to R2F
	A		Analyst software level req. are revealed by analysts as direct requirements aiming at offering some need for service, user support, or development support, a quality property, or a compliance constraint
		1	– Software req. – Functional req. – Data req. – User interface req. – Technical interface req. – Operation req. – Process support for operation req. – Human support for operation req. – Software support for operation req. – Hardware support for operation req. – Cognitive context for operation req.

Analyst req.			– Development req. – Process support for development req. – Human support for development req. – Software support for development req. – Hardware support for development req. – Cognitive context for development req.
		2	– Quality req. – Functional adequation req. – Performance req. – Interoperability req. – Usability req. – Reliability req. – Security req. – Maintainability req. – Portability req. – Compliance req. – Management req. – Technology req. – Economics req. – Culture req. – Social req. – Political req. – Legal req.
	B	Analyst system level req. are revealed by analysts as indirect requirements aiming at supporting a given system activity. So, they are left to designers and developers to make them specific as a first step toward the solution	
		1	Analyst, endogenous, system level req. Same categorization as analyst, endogenous, software level req. (A-1)
		2	Analyst, exogenous, system level req. Same categorization as analyst, exogenous, software level req. (A-2)
	C	Analyst business level req. are revealed by analysts as indirect requirements aiming at satisfying a given business goal. So, they are left to designers and developers to make them specific as a first step toward the solution	
		1	Analyst, endogenous, business level req. Same categorization as analyst, endogenous, software level req. (A-1)
		2	Analyst, exogenous, business level req. Same categorization as analyst, exogenous, software level req. (A-2)

Table 5.6. *New hybrid categorization proposed in the SMART approach. A: software level req.; B: system level req.; C: business level req.; 1: endogenous Req.; 2: exogenous Req.*

6

Operationalization

The purpose of this chapter is to operationalize the SMART approach. Operationalization allows us to shift from the abstract aspects of our approach to concrete aspects. In the context of our study, it can be defined as the transformation process of the abstract concepts of our approach, which are linked to the new reference framework, and the new hybrid requirements categorization into two operating models for requirements engineering and management.

Based on Requirements Metadata Language (RML) (Chikh 2017), the first model can be used to qualify requirements according to several predefined categories of metadata. The second model, which concerns the requirements themselves, allows for a multi-view representation of all the categories resulting from the hybrid requirements categorization.

6.1. New requirements metadata model

In this section, we propose a scheme for the qualification of requirements. In recent years, requirements qualification, which has become an important issue, must be appropriately taken into account. It improves the productivity of the requirements engineering process. Indeed, the intensive use of requirements throughout the software life cycle makes it very strategic information. Individual requirements act as fragments of information that

For a color version of all the figures in this chapter, see www.iste.co.uk/chikh/smart.zip.

include a semantic dimension, supported by the use of metadata. In this perspective, producing, sharing and reusing requirements between several software projects within distributed environments have become a necessary activity and raise new challenges.

Metadata provides the context for finding, analyzing, verifying and validating requirements. Without these metadata, it would be almost impossible to use the requirements in a rational way. In order to qualify requirements with metadata, certain vocabularies are needed. In this section, we present the structure of RML that we proposed in Chikh (2017) and that we adapt to the R2F framework and the hybrid categorization proposed in the previous chapter.

It corresponds to the building block of the metadata schema presented in Haslhofer and Klas (2010).

The RML structure is primarily based on LOM, a standard that specifies the syntax and semantics of the metadata of learning objects, defined as the attributes required to describe a learning object (IEEE 2002). In fact, the RML data model is structured as a hierarchy, comprising categories, aggregated data elements and simple data elements, which represent leaf nodes. Only simple data elements have individual values defined by their corresponding value space and data type. All data elements are optional. A data element can contain a list of ordered or unordered values, rather than a single value. A vocabulary, which is a recommended list of appropriate values, could be assigned to certain data elements.

Table 6.1 shows the basic RML schema identifying the categories and their integrated data elements, their explanation and their corresponding value space. The "general", "life cycle", "technical" and "annotation" categories are almost similar to their corresponding categories in LOM. Nevertheless, their content has been adapted to the requirements. Finally, the three categories "specification", "traceability" and "taxonomy", which are highly field-dependent, have been completely reformulated to satisfy the requirements. The metadata for the latter categories is described below.

No.	Name	Explanation	Value space/example
1	General	This category groups the general information that describes the requirement.	
1.1	Identifier	Requirement identifier.	Possible codification of the identifier: UA level: U for user requirement, A for analyst requirement; + BS2 level: B for business, S for system, L for software; + E2 category: D for enDogenous, X for eXogenous; + Sequential number of the requirement.
1.2	Language	Primary natural language of the requirement.	English, French, Arabic, etc.
1.3	Software project	Software project title or reference.	
1.4	Appendix	Requirement appendix reference.	URL; URI; bookmark.
2	Life cycle	This category describes the history and current state of the requirement.	
2.1	Version	Requirement version number. It makes it possible to keep track of all the possible versions of the requirement.	
2.2	Status	Requirement completion status.	Draft; revised; valid.
2.3	Contribution	All contributions to the state of the requirement during its life cycle.	
2.3.1	Contribution role	Nature of contribution to the state of the requirement.	Elicitation; specification; verification; validation.
2.3.2	Contribution actor	Reference of the contributor to the state of the requirement.	

2.3.3	Contribution date	Date of contribution to the state of the requirement.	
3	Technical	This category describes the technical characteristics of the appendix of the requirement.	
3.1	Format	Technical data type(s) of the appendix of the requirement.	MIME types or "non-digital".
3.2	Size	This data element shall refer to the size of the appendix of the requirement.	
4	Specification	This category describes the key semantic characteristics of the requirement.	
4.1	Style	Requirement style used to represent its content in the appendix.	Data model; data dictionary; data expression; virtual windows; context diagrams; event list.
4.2	Representation	Requirement representation according to Glinz (2005).	Operational; quantitative; qualitative; declarative.
4.3	Role	Requirement role according to Glinz (2005).	Prescriptive; descriptive; assumptive.
4.4	Satisfaction	Requirement satisfaction according to Glinz (2005).	Soft; hard.
4.5	Derivation	Requirement derivation. How the requirement was obtained?	Primary; interpreted; derived.
4.6	Granularity	Requirement granularity. The requirement may range from a high-level abstract statement of a service to a detailed mathematical functional specification.	1: requirement is typically "atomic"; 2: requirement can include level 1 requirement; 3: requirement can include level 2 requirement.
4.7	Reusability	Requirement reusability.	Completely; partially; no.
4.8	Priority	Requirement priority.	High; medium; low.
4.9	Risk	Requirement risk.	High; medium; low.

4.10	Difficulty	Requirement difficulty.	High; medium; low.
4.11	Stability	Requirement stability.	High; medium; low.
5	Traceability	This category describes the relationships of the requirement with other requirements, sources and artifacts.	
5.1	Other requirement	Reference link to another requirement.	
5.1.1	Other requirement reference	Reference of the other requirement.	
5.1.2	Relation type	Relationship type of the requirement with the other requirement.	Alternativity; dependency; refinement; evolution; satisfiability; overlap; conflict; rationalization.
5.2	Source	Reference link to a requirement source.	
5.2.1	Source reference	Reference of the requirement source.	
5.2.2	Source type	Type of the requirement source.	Regulation; contract; standard; user.
5.3	Design artifact	Reference link to a related design artifact.	
5.3.1	Artifact reference	Reference of the corresponding design artifact of the requirement.	
5.3.2	Artifact type	Type of the corresponding design artifact of the requirement.	Class diagram; state machine diagram; sequence diagram.
5.4	Subject	Requirement subject according to the reference framework.	
5.4.1	Generic subject	Generic requirement subject according to the reference framework.	"Software"; "operation environment"; "development environment" subjects and their descendants.

5.4.2	Specific subject	Specific requirement subject according to the real software project.	
5.5	Factor	Requirement factor according to the reference framework.	
5.5.1	Generic factor	Generic requirement factor according to the reference framework.	"Quality" and "compliance" factors, and their descendants.
5.5.2	Specific factor	Specific requirement factor according to the real software project.	
6	Annotation	This category provides comments on the use of the requirement and information on when and by whom the comments were created.	
6.1	Annotation entity	Author of the annotation.	
6.2	Annotation date	Creation date of the annotation.	
6.3	Annotation description	Annotation content. It could be used for communication between stakeholders.	
7	Taxonomy	This category is intended to be used for classifying the requirement.	
7.1	UA level	Requirement level according to the UA scale.	User; analyst.
7.2	BS2 level	Requirement level according to the BS2 scale.	Business; system; software.
7.3	E2 category	Requirement category according to the E2 taxonomy.	Endogenous; exogenous.
7.4	Nature	Requirement nature. It represents a generalization of the kind facet of Glinz (2005).	See Figure 5.13.
7.5	Application domain	Application domain of the software project.	Sales; manufacturing; accounting; car safety.

Table 6.1. *Basic RML schema adapted to the R2F framework and the hybrid categorization*

"Specification"

– Style (Metadata 4.1): refers to the style used to represent the requirement such as a data model, a data dictionary, data expression and virtual windows for data needs such as context diagrams, the list of events and use cases for functional requirements.

– Representation (Metadata 4.2): refers to the mode used to represent the requirement, which can assume one of the following values: "operational", "quantitative", "qualitative" and "declarative", proposed by Glinz (2005).

– Role (Metadata 4.3): refers to the role played by the requirement, which can assume one of the following values: "prescriptive", "descriptive" and "assumptive", proposed by Glinz (2005).

– Satisfaction (Metadata 4.4): refers to satisfying the requirement, which can assume one of the following values: "soft" and "hard", proposed by Glinz (2005).

– Derivation (Metadata 4.5): shows how the requirement has been derived. It can assume one of the following values: "primary", "interpreted" and "derived".

– Granularity (Metadata 4.6): the requirement can range from a service or constraint high-level abstract declaration to a detailed mathematical functional specification.

– Reusability (Metadata 4.7): it is interesting to analyze which requirements within software projects are fully or partially reusable. In fact, while generic requirements can be reused without any modification, more specific requirements may require efforts to adapt to the context.

– Priority (Metadata 4.8): refers to the requirement priority in relation to the customer, which can assume one of the following values: "high", "medium" and "low".

– Risk (Metadata 4.9): refers to the estimated technical risk of the requirement, which can assume one of the following values: "high", "medium" and "low".

– Difficulty (Metadata 4.10): refers to the estimated technical difficulty in implementing the requirement, which can assume one of the following values: "high", "medium" and "low".

– Stability (Metadata 4.11): refers to the stability (maturity) of the requirement in relation to the customer, which can assume one of the following values: "high", "medium" and "low".

"Traceability"

– Other requirement (Metadata 5.1): makes it possible to link the requirement to other requirements according to different types of relationships such as alternativity, dependency, refinement, evolution, satisfiability, overlapping, conflict and rationalization (Ramesh and Jarke 2001).

– Source (Metadata 5.2): refers to the notion of pre-traceability relationships (Gotel and Finkelstein 1994). It includes the relationships between requirements and the sources that have generated them, such as the regulation, contract, standard and software project.

– Design artifact (Metadata 5.3): concerns the notion of post-traceability relationships (Gotel and Finkelstein 1994). It includes the relationships between requirements and design artifacts, which are created in the architectural and detailed design, such as the class diagram, state machine diagram and sequence diagram.

– Generic subject (Metadata 5.4.1): refers to the generic requirement subject according to R2F.

– Specific subject (Metadata 5.4.2): refers to the specific requirement subject.

– Generic factor (Metadata 5.5.1): refers to the generic requirement factor according to R2F.

– Specific factor (Metadata 5.5.2): refers to the specific requirement factor.

"Taxonomy"

– UA level (Metadata 7.1 in RML): refers to the requirement level according to the UA scale, as described in section 5.3.1. It can assume one of the following values: "user" and "analyst".

– BS2 level (Metadata 7.2 in RML): refers to the requirement level according to the BS2 scale, as described in section 5.3.2. It can assume one of the following values: "business", "system" and "software".

– E2 category (Metadata 7.3 in RML): refers to the category of the requirement according to the E2 taxonomy, as described in section 5.3.3. It can assume one of the following two values: "endogenous" or "exogenous".

– Nature (Metadata 7.4 in RML): refers to the nature of the requirement according to the taxonomy proposed in Figure 5.13, and described in section 5.3.4.

– Application domain (Metadata 7.5 in RML): refers to the application domain of the corresponding software project such as sales, purchasing or accounting.

Figure 6.1 shows the seven categories of metadata in the RML base schema.

Metadata can be used in information retrieval and in calculating similarity between requirements. In order to simplify the use of the RML language, we propose a minimal application profile, called "RML-bis", covering the most important aspects of the requirements in the SMART approach. RML-bis is composed of the following list of metadata, selected from the seven RML categories: 1.1 Identifier; 1.3 Software project; 1.4 Appendix; 2.2 Status; 4.1 Style; 4.2 Representation; 4.3 Role; 4.4 Satisfaction; 4.7 Reusability; 4.8 Priority; 4.11 Stability; 5.1 Other requirement (5.1.1 Other requirement reference and 5.1.2 Relation type); 5.2 Source (5.2.1 Source reference and 5.2.2 Source type); 5.3 Design artifact (5.3.1 Artifact reference and 5.3.2 Artifact type); 5.4 Subject (5.4.1 Generic subject and 5.4.2 Specific subject); 5.5 Factor (5.5.1 Generic factor and 5.5.2 Specific factor); 7.1 UA level; 7.2 BS2 level; 7.3 E2 category; 7.4 Nature; 7.5 Application domain. Finally, it should be noted that some metadata are indicated during requirements elicitation, while others are indicated during other engineering activities such as analysis or validation, as shown in section 7.2.

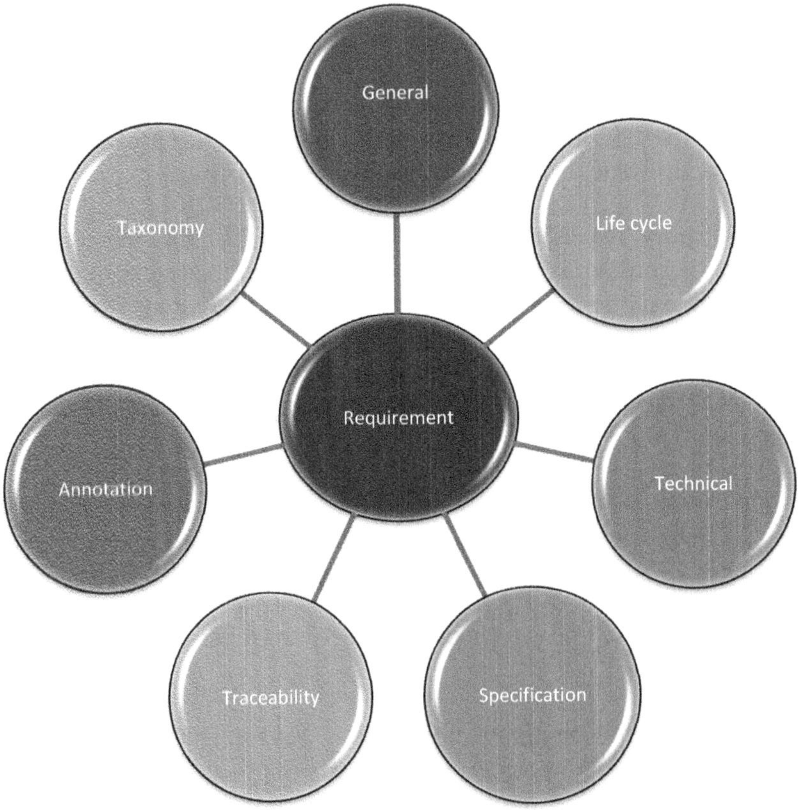

Figure 6.1. *Requirements qualification*

6.2. New requirements model

In this section, we first propose a requirement structure, which is based on the R2F framework and the hybrid categorization, proposed in the previous chapter. Next, we propose a multi-view model of requirements that supports the representation of all possible categories of requirements.

The new requirement structure consists of the following triplet (see Figure 6.2):

– a requirement statement, which follows a corresponding view of the requirement model, chosen based on the categorization attributes of the requirement, namely, the category (endogenous or exogenous) and the BS2 level of requirement, on the one hand, and the requirement priority, on the other hand;

– a requirement descriptor, which contains a number of metadata elements (attributes) of the RML language presented in section 6.1, and which characterizes several aspects of a requirement. The identifier, which is the most important descriptor attribute, is mandatory. It is used to uniquely designate a requirement, thus distinguishing it from other requirements;

– a fit criterion, which specifies how the software successfully satisfies this requirement.

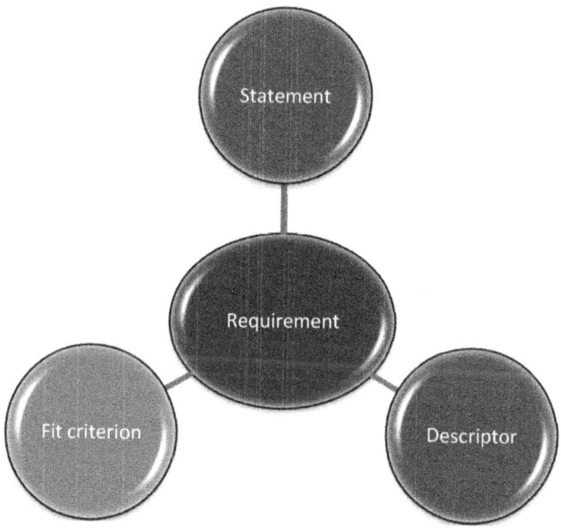

Figure 6.2. *Requirement structure*

In turn, the requirement statement is structured in the form of the next triplet (see Figure 6.3):

– an (optional) introduction, which defines the context for justifying and/or introducing the requirement;

– a (mandatory) body, which represents the core of the declaration, formulated according to the model associated with it. It consists of the following five elements: (1) an instruction formula that changes according to the priority and importance of the requirement; (2) a generic subject requirement chosen from R2F; (3) a specific requirement subject introduced by the analyst; (4) a generic requirement factor chosen from R2F; and (5) a specific requirement factor introduced by the analyst. Elements 4 and 5 relate only to exogenous requirements;

– an (optional) appendix, which contains the details of the statement in a well-defined specification language (style): informal (natural language), semi-formal (graphic) or formal (mathematical).

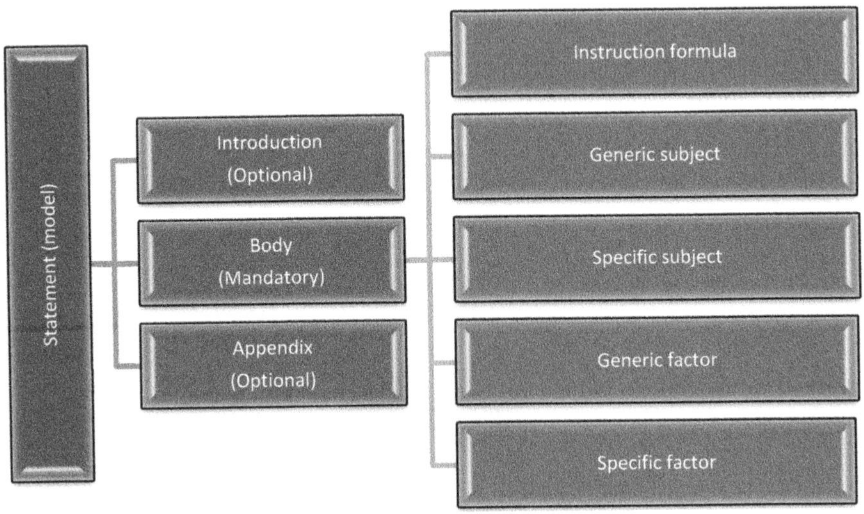

Figure 6.3. *Requirement statement structure*

The V6 multi-view model (six views), which consists of a view for each category, is proposed by the new hybrid categorization requirements approach (Table 5.6). More specifically, it concerns the "analyst" requirements. In fact, the "user" level requirements do not generally follow a predefined model.

Table 6.2 shows the V6 multi-view model of the requirements:

– The first three views of this model – DB, DSy and DSo – are related to the three levels of the BS2 scale of endogenous requirements.

– The second three views of this model – XB, XSy and XSo – are related to the three levels of the BS2 scale of exogenous requirements.

E2	BS2	View
EnDogenous	Business	DB: The "software_name" software (should/shall/must) (ensure/require/adopt) the necessary ("GS selected from R2F") to satisfy the following "specific business goal_statement" business goal.
	System	DSy: The "software_name" software (should/shall/must) (ensure/require/adopt) the necessary ("GS selected from R2F") to support the following "specific operation activity_statement" operation activity.
	Software	DSo: The "software_name" software (should/shall/must) (ensure/require/adopt) ("GS selected from R2F") ["SS_name"] [described as follows: "SS_statement"] [according to the model: "SS_model"].
EXogenous	Business	XB: The ("software_name" software)/("GS selected from R2F": "SS_name") (should/shall/must) ensure the necessary "GF selected from R2F" to satisfy the following "specific business goal_statement" business goal.
	System	XSy: The ("software_name" software)/("GS selected from R2F": "SS_name") (should/shall/must) ensure the necessary "GF selected from R2F" to support the following "specific operation activity_statement" operation activity.
	Software	XSo: The ("software_name" software)/("GS selected from R2F": "SS_name") (should/shall/must) ensure "GF selected from R2F" as follows: "SF_statement".

Table 6.2. *New V6 requirements model*

Three alternative expressions characterize this model:

– The first expression "ensure", which is used by both endogenous and exogenous views, concerns, for the former, the four GS of R2F, related to "function", "data", "user interface", and "technical interface", comprised of the GS "software", and for the latter, all the GF of R2F.

– The second expression "require", which is used exclusively by endogenous views, concerns the four GS of R2F, related to "procedural support", "human support", "software support" and "hardware support", comprised of the two GS of R2F "operation environment" and "development environment".

– The third expression "adopt", which is exclusively used by endogenous views, concerns the two GS of R2F, related to "cognitive context", comprised of the two GS "operation environment" and "development environment".

The expression "according to the model", specific to the DSo view, is used by the design requirements, which are proposed in section 5.3.2.

We are now presenting a nomenclature of requirements categories that includes all the categories proposed by the new hybrid requirements categorization approach (see Table 5.6), according to the new V6 requirement model.

This nomenclature is limited to the "analyst" requirements. The "user-level" requirements do not generally comply with a predefined model. The categories of this nomenclature are first classified according to the E2 (endogenous, exogenous) taxonomy, and then according to the BS2 scale (business, system and software).

We present a set of cards in the Appendix that describe the categories of this nomenclature. Each card specifies the corresponding requirements categories (see Table 5.6), the corresponding view of the V6 model with its version adapted to the previous categories and finally an example of a requirement with its RML-bis descriptor.

6.2.1. *Endogenous requirements*

The purpose of this section is to present the categories of the endogenous requirements through the three levels of the BS2 scale.

A set of cards in the Appendix describes these categories in accordance with the three endogenous views of the V6 model (see Table 6.3).

BS2	View	Card numbers
Business	DB: The "software_name" software (should/shall/must) (ensure/require/adopt) the necessary ("GS selected from R2F") to satisfy the following "specific business goal_statement" business goal.	1, 2, 3
System	DSy: The "software_name" software (should/shall/must) (ensure/require/adopt) the necessary ("GS selected from R2F") to support the following "specific operation activity_statement" operation activity.	4, 5, 6
Software	DSo: The "software_name" software (should/shall/must) (ensure/require/adopt) ("GS selected from R2F") [: "SS_name"] [described as follows: "SS_statement"] [according to the model: "SS_model"].	7–29

Table 6.3. *New V6 requirements model – endogenous views*

6.2.1.1. *Business-level requirements*

Endogenous business-level requirements characterize the three subjects "software", "operation environment" and "development environment" and their descendants by linking them to the "goal" subject from the "cognitive context for operation" subject, which itself is from the "operation environment" subject.

Cards 1–3 provide adapted versions of the "DB" view of the V6 model using the "ensure", "require" and "adopt" options, respectively.

6.2.1.2. *System-level requirements*

Endogenous system-level requirements characterize the three subjects "software", "operation environment" and "development environment" and their descendants by linking them to the "operation activity" subject from the "process support for operation" subject itself from the "operation environment" subject.

Cards 4–6 provide adapted versions of the "DSy" view of the V6 model using the "ensure", "require" and "adopt" options, respectively.

6.2.1.3. *Software-level requirements*

Endogenous software-level requirements characterize the three subjects "software", "operation environment" and "development environment" and their descendants, describing them directly.

6.2.1.3.1. Software requirements

Software requirements describe the intrinsic aspects of the future software. They consist of the following four categories of requirements: (1) functional, (2) data, (3) user interface and (4) technical interface.

Cards 7, 9, 11 and 13, which concern "function", "data", "user interface" and "technical interface", provide adapted versions of the "DSo" view of the V6 model using the "ensure" option.

Cards 8, 10, 12 and 14, which concern the design aspect of "function", "data", "user interface" and "technical interface", provide adapted versions of the "DSo" view of the V6 model using the "ensure" and "according to the model" options.

Design requirements

As we pointed out at the beginning of section 5.3.2, we consider the "design" level of the "goal–design" scale as a particular type of the "software" level of our scale; more specifically software requirements, in which requirements are expressed in terms of "how". However, unlike the Lauesen scale, which at this level merely considers user interfaces, we extend this particular type to the four software aspects, namely, "function", "data", "user interface" and "technical interface".

In fact, we consider that software requirements become design requirements when they include choices involving design elements, such as screenshots for the "user interface" subject, database schemas for the "data" subject, algorithms for the "function" subject and finally communication protocols for the "technical interface" subject.

Functional requirements

These involve identifying and specifying the functions of the future software, for example by specifying a list of their names.

Design-type functional requirements

A design-type functional requirement, which reflects a particular case of a functional requirement, is expressed in the form of an algorithm or any other design model.

Data requirements

These involve identifying and specifying all the domain data to be stored by the software, regardless of their function, by specifying a list of names of the type entities (classes) of these data.

Design-type data requirements

A design-type data requirement, which reflects a particular case of a data requirement, is expressed in the form of a database schema or any other design model.

User interface requirements

These include identifying and specifying the human–machine interfaces of the future software by specifying a list of names of these user interfaces. These requirements, which can also be considered as a particular case of functional requirements, have the specificity of focusing on the communication aspect of the future software with the user. It can also be said that they consist of specifying the functions of the future software whose main mission is only to interact with the user, either in consultation mode, in update mode in the broad sense of the term (creation, modification or deletion) or in hybrid mode. It would then be interesting to also specify the link with the requirement to which they are related. It should be noted that while these requirements can be provided in the form of screenshots. In this case, they correspond to "design-level" requirements (Lauesen 2002) described in section 3.3.4.

Design-type user interface requirements

A design-type user interface requirement, which reflects a particular case of user interface requirements, is expressed in the form of a screenshot or any other design model.

Technical interface requirements

These involve identifying and specifying the interfaces of the future software with other software by specifying a list of names of the technical interfaces of these other software programs. The distinct specificity of these requirements, which can also be considered as a particular case of functional requirements, is that they focus on the communication aspect of the future software with other software. It can also be said that they consist of specifying functions of the future software whose main mission is merely to exchange with other software in either direction. It would then be interesting to also specify the link with the requirement to which they are related.

Design-type technical interface requirements

A design requirement for a design-type technical interface, which is a particular case of the technical interface requirements, is expressed in the form of a communication protocol or any other design model.

6.2.1.3.2. Operation requirements

The operation requirements describe the aspects of the future software related to its operation. They consist of the following five categories of requirements: (1) operation procedural support, (2) operation human support, (3) operation software support, (4) operation hardware support and (5) cognitive context of the operation process.

Cards 15–18, which concern the subjects related to the operation support of type "process", "human", "software" and "hardware", provide adapted versions of the "DSo" view of the V6 model using the "require" option.

Cards 19–21, which concern the subjects related to the operation cognitive context, namely, "concept", "goal" and "rule", provide adapted versions of the V6 model "DSo" view using the "adopt" option.

Operation procedural support requirements

These involve identifying and specifying the operation activities of the whole system that the software must support, assist or drive by specifying their list.

Operation human support requirements

These involve identifying and specifying the profiles of the different end users (employees and external actors) by specifying a list of their categories.

Operation software support requirements

This involves identifying and specifying the new software platform required to run the software by specifying the list of potential operating systems, the list of databases, the list of other software, the existing data in the current software (for the transition), the list of social media and the documentation list.

Operation hardware support requirements

This involves identifying and specifying the new hardware platform required to run the software by specifying the list of computers (servers) with their hardware configuration (CPU, storage units and input/output units), the equipment necessary for the computer network, as well as other digital devices (sensors, actuators and other devices) required by the software.

Cognitive context requirements of the operation process

The operation cognitive context requirements, which are not requirements in the strict sense, consist of the following three categories of requirements: (1) concepts, (2) goals and (3) rules.

Domain concepts requirements

These involve identifying and defining the concepts of the underlying domain of the future software by specifying a list of names of these concepts.

Business goal requirements

These involve identifying and defining the business goals that the company is trying to achieve through the different systems implemented, and which can represent tangible gains by specifying a tree structure of these business goals.

Business rule requirements

These involve identifying and defining the business rules to be applied by the future software by specifying a list of these business rules or the functions they support. These are not requirements as such.

6.2.1.3.3. Development requirements

Development requirements describe the aspects of the future software related to its development. They consist of the following five categories of requirements: (1) development procedural support, (2) development human support, (3) development software support, (4) development hardware support and (5) cognitive context of the development process.

The five categories of development requirements are illustrated with examples that are consistent with the DSo view of the V6 model.

Cards 22–25, which concern subjects related to development support of "process", "human", "software" and "hardware", provide adapted versions of the "DSo" view of the V6 model using the "require" option.

Cards 26–29, which concern subjects related to the development of cognitive context, namely, "architecture", "methods", "technical" and "artifacts", provide adapted versions of the "DSo" view of the V6 model using the "adopt" option.

Development procedural support requirements

These involve identifying and specifying the various recommended activities of its development cycle such as analysis, general design, detailed design and implementation.

Development human support requirements

These involve identifying and specifying the different categories of developers of the future software – analysts, designers, programmers and testers – by formulating a list of their categories.

Development software support requirements

These involve identifying and specifying the new software platform needed for software development by specifying the CASE (Computer Aided Software Environment) tools, the IDE (Integrated Development Environment), the programming language required by the developer for the development of the software or any other development software.

Development hardware support requirements

These involve identifying and specifying the new hardware platform required for software development, identifying the computer with its hardware configuration (CPU, storage units and input/output units) as well as other digital devices (sensors, actuators and other devices) required for the software development.

Cognitive context requirements of the development process

The development cognitive context requirements consist of the following four categories of requirements: (1) architecture, (2) methods, (3) techniques and (4) artifacts.

Architecture requirements

These involve identifying and specifying the recommended choice of the future software architecture, such as MVC, 3-tier and SOA.

Methods requirements

These involve identifying and specifying the recommended choice of methods for the development of the future software, such as Merise, Remora and OMT.

Techniques requirements

These involve identifying and specifying the recommended choice of development techniques for the future software, such as interviews, observation and prototyping.

Artifacts requirements

These involve identifying and specifying the recommended choice of the different development artifacts of the future software, such as class diagrams, activity diagrams, sequence diagrams or test plans.

6.2.2. *Exogenous requirements*

The purpose of this section is to present the categories of the exogenous requirements through the three levels of the BS2 scale.

A set of cards in the Appendix describe these categories in accordance with the three exogenous views of the V6 model (see Table 6.4).

BS2	View	Card numbers
Business	XB: The ("software_name" software)/("GS selected from R2F": "SS_name") (should/shall/must) ensure the necessary "GF selected from R2F" to satisfy the following "specific business goal_statement" business goal.	30 (Quality) 31 (Compliance)
System	XSy: The ("software_name" software)/("GS selected from R2F": "SS_name") (should/shall/must) ensure the necessary "GF selected from R2F" to support the following "specific operation activity_statement" operation activity.	32 (Quality) 33 (Compliance)
Software	XSo: The ("software_name" software)/("GS selected from R2F": "SS_name") (should/shall/must) ensure "GF selected from R2F" as follows: "SF_statement".	34–41 (Quality) 42–48 (Compliance)

Table 6.4. *New V6 requirements model – exogenous views*

6.2.2.1. *Business-level requirements*

Exogenous business-level requirements characterize the three subjects, "software", "operation environment" and "development environment" and their descendants, by linking them to the "goal" subject from the "cognitive context for operation" subject that itself derives from the "operation environment" subject. They concern the application of the requirement factors on these subjects.

Cards 30 and 31, which concern quality and compliance factors, provide adapted versions of the "XB" view of the V6 model using the "ensure" option.

6.2.2.1.1. Quality requirements

Exogenous business-level requirements, related to quality, consist of the following eight categories of requirements: (1) functional adequation, (2) performance, (3) interoperability, (4) usability, (5) reliability, (6) security, (7) maintainability and (8) portability.

6.2.2.1.2. Compliance requirements

Exogenous business-level requirements, related to compliance, consist of the following seven categories of requirements: (1) managerial, (2) technological, (3) economic, (4) cultural, (5) social, (6) political and (7) legal.

6.2.2.2. *System-level requirements*

Exogenous system-level requirements characterize the three subjects “software”, “operation environment” and “development environment” and their descendants by linking them to the “operation activity” subject from the “process support for operation” subject that itself derived from the “operation environment” subject. They concern the application of the requirement factors to these subjects.

Cards 32 and 33, which concern quality and compliance factors, provide adapted versions of the “XSy” view of the V6 model using the “ensure” option.

6.2.2.2.1. Quality requirements

System-level exogenous requirements, related to quality, consist of the following eight categories of requirements: (1) functional adequation, (2) performance, (3) interoperability, (4) usability, (5) reliability, (6) security, (7) maintainability and (8) portability.

6.2.2.2.2. Compliance requirements

System-level exogenous compliance requirements consist of the following seven categories of requirements: (1) managerial, (2) technological, (3) economic, (4) cultural, (5) social, (6) political and (7) legal.

6.2.2.3. *Software-level requirements*

Exogenous software-level requirements characterize the three subjects “software”, “operation environment” and “development environment” and their descendants directly describing them. They concern the application of the requirement factors to these subjects. They include both software quality and its compliance with its interdisciplinary environment.

6.2.2.3.1. Quality requirements

Software-level exogenous requirements, related to quality, consist of the following eight categories of requirements: (1) functional adequation, (2) performance, (3) interoperability, (4) usability, (5) reliability, (6) security, (7) maintainability and (8) portability.

Cards 34–31, which concern quality factors, provide adapted versions of the "XSo" view of the V6 model using the "ensure" option.

Functional adequation requirements

These requirements involve specifying the degree to which the future software provides the functions that satisfy the expressed and implicit needs under specified operating conditions. The concerned requirement subject is "function" from the "software" subject.

Performance requirements

These involve specifying the performance of the future software with respect to the resources employed under determined conditions. The concerned requirement subject is "software" or each of its descendants.

Interoperability requirements

These involve specifying the degree to which the future software can exchange information with other software and/or perform its functions, while sharing the same hardware and software environments. The concerned requirement subject is "software" or each of its descendants.

Usability requirements

These involve specifying the degree to which the future software can be used to achieve the identified goals effectively, efficiently and satisfactorily, within a specified context. The concerned requirement subject is "user interface" from the "software" subject.

Reliability requirements

These involve specifying the degree to which the future software performs the specified functions, under specified conditions, for a specified period of time. The requirement subject concerned is "software" or each of its descendants.

Security requirements

These involve specifying the degree to which the future software protects information and data, such that people or other software have access to them that corresponds to their authorization level. The concerned requirement subject is “software” or each of its descendants.

Maintainability requirements

These involve specifying the degree of effectiveness and efficiency to which the future software can be modified by the authorized persons. The concerned requirement subject is “software” or each of its descendants.

Portability requirements

These involve specifying the degree of effectiveness and efficiency to which the future software can be transferred from one hardware or software environment to another, or from one use to another (reusability). The concerned requirement subject is “software” or each of its descendants.

6.2.2.3.2. Compliance requirements

The software-level exogenous requirements concerning compliance consist of the following seven categories of requirements: (1) managerial, (2) technological, (3) economic, (4) cultural, (5) social, (6) political and (7) legal.

Cards 42–48, which concern compliance factors, provide adapted versions of the “XSo” view of thc V6 model using the “ensure” option.

Managerial requirements

These involve specifying the managerial requirements which concern, among other things, the following terms:

– payment terms relating to the R2F “Payment” compliance factor, specifying a threshold that must not be exceeded;

– delivery terms relating to the R2F “Delivery” compliance factor, specifying, for example, in the case of the software itself, a list of deliverables, one executable code, source code, user documentation, technical documentation, commercial documentation and the type of delivery (partial or total);

– training terms relating to the R2F "Training" compliance factor, specifying, for example, the purpose of the training, the concerned users, the level of qualification sought after as well as the prerequisites;

– testing terms relating to the R2F "Testing" compliance factor, specifying the types of tests to be performed and the test sets to be used (real or fictitious data);

– installation terms relating to the R2F "Installation" compliance factor, specifying the installation deadline and who is responsible for the installation (the user with or without assistance, and the developer);

– transition terms relating to the R2F "Transition" compliance factor, which concerns the transition from the old software to the future software, specifying the data from the old software to be converted to the new format, who is responsible for conversion and the type of transition (direct, a period of simultaneity).

Technological requirements

These involve specifying the technological requirements which concern, among other things, the following terms:

– trending terms relating to the R2F "Trending" compliance factor, specifying, for example, the new technological trends to be considered in the deployment of future software, such as cloud computing, grid computing, distributed computing, cluster computing, time-sharing computing, client-server computing, peer-to-peer computing and mobile computing;

– standard terms relating to the R2F "Standard" compliance factor, specifying the new standards and protocols to be considered for the development of the future software, such as Universal Design, Discovery and Integration (UDDI), Web Service Description Language (WSDL), Web Services Inspection Language (WSIL), SOAP and Web Services Interoperability (WS-I).

Economic requirements

These involve specifying the economic requirements concerning, among other things, the following terms:

– cost terms relating to the R2F "Cost" compliance factor, specifying the costs of developing and using the future software;

– income terms relating to the R2F “Income” compliance factor, specifying the expected income from the use of the future software.

Cultural requirements

These involve specifying the cultural requirements which concern, among other things, the following terms:

– appearance terms relating to the R2F “Look and feel” compliance factor, specifying the intended appearance, simplicity and the formal nature of the interface of the future software;

– language terms relating to the R2F “Language” compliance factor, specifying the language of the user interfaces and printed reports used by the future software;

– belief terms relating to the R2F “Believe” compliance factor, specifying the values, preferences and taboos used by the future software;

– ethical terms relating to the R2F “Ethic” compliance factor, specifying the use of cookies and other technical options used by the future software;

– currency terms relating to the R2F “Currency” compliance factor, specifying the different currencies used by the future software;

– metrics terms relating to the R2F “Metric” compliance factor, specifying the different units of measurement used by the future software;

– format terms relating to the R2F “Format” compliance factor, specifying the different formats of dates, hours, telephone numbers and amounts used by the future software.

Social requirements

These involve specifying the social requirements which concern, among other things, the following terms:

– cooperation terms relating to the R2F “Cooperation” compliance factor, specifying the collaborative work with the future software;

– sharing terms relating to the R2F “Sharing” compliance factor, specifying file sharing between users with the future software.

Political requirements

These involve specifying the political requirements which concern, among other things, the following terms:

– adhesion terms relating to the R2F "Adhesion" compliance factor, specifying the adhesion of syndicates to the future software;

– conflict resolution terms relating to the R2F "Conflict resolution" compliance factor, specifying the resolution of conflicts between stakeholders of the future software.

Legal requirements

These involve specifying the legal requirements which concern, among other things, the following terms:

– intellectual property terms relating to the R2F "Intellectual property" compliance factor, specifying the intellectual property of the future software;

– regulation terms relating to the R2F "Regulation" compliance factor, specifying the regulation aspects related to the future software;

– legislation terms relating to the R2F "Legislation" compliance factor, specifying the aspects of existing laws (internal or external to the company) related to the future software.

7

Usage

The purpose of this chapter is to present the objectives of the SMART approach and illustrate its use with scenarios by type of engineering activity. We use the term "element" below to refer to an R2F GS or GF.

7.1. Objectives

Through R2F and its V6 model, the SMART approach aims to support:

– analysts or requirements engineers to better:

- elicit the new "analyst-level" requirements by *ex nihilo* creation, reusing existing "analyst-level" requirements or reusing requirements patterns,

- specify the new "analyst-level" requirements in accordance with the V6 model views, specific to each category of requirements, and to the nomenclature tree that may be preceded by the natural tree structure of the software application domain,

- analyze the "analyst-level" requirements: completeness analysis, first in terms of coverage of the generic and specific R2F elements, by the "user-level" requirements and then in terms of coverage of the latter by those at the "analyst-level"; consistency and conflict analysis; multidimensional analysis whose goal is to know the distribution of requirements according to different criteria extracted from R2F and the new categorization,

- validate the "analyst-level" requirements,

- qualify the requirements: metadata qualification and multi-criteria research, qualification of relationships with other requirements and other artifacts of the future software;

– developers on the one hand and customers on the other hand to:

- increase their collective knowledge of software requirements, with R2F, V6 and the concepts associated with them,

- standardize their narrative using a simple, precise and unified vocabulary.

7.2. Usage scenarios

In order to facilitate the use of the SMART approach and to encourage requirements reuse, we attach to each category of requirements in the nomenclature typical requirements that represent patterns for the requirements of that category. These patterns are either designed by experts in the field or extracted from the literature. A library of patterns is provided for this purpose.

Some pairs of categories in the nomenclature also exhibit potential dependencies between their respective requirements, such as the two pairs: technical interface requirements versus operation software support requirements, and functional requirements versus business rules requirements.

Other pairs of categories in the nomenclature also exhibit potential links of natural conflict between their respective requirements, such as the pair: usability requirements versus security requirements.

Furthermore, the requirements from previous projects are associated in two ways. First, they are linked to the categories of the UA and BS2 scales, as well as the E2 and by-nature taxonomies, through their qualification using the corresponding metadata from RML-bis (7.1 UA-level, 7.2 BS2-level, 7.3 E2 category and 7.4 Nature). Second, they are linked to the generic and specific elements of R2F via their qualification through the corresponding metadata from RML-bis (5.4.1 Generic subject, 5.4.2 Specific subject, 5.5.1 Generic factor and 5.5.2 Specific factor).

We plan to use the SMART approach through several potential scenarios that translate the core requirements engineering and management activities.

7.2.1. *Elicitation activity*

We present two different scenarios that illustrate how the SMART approach is used in the elicitation activity:

– In the first scenario, the SMART approach aims to support the elicitation process, from scratch or by re-using similar requirements, of a new "analyst-level" requirement, to meet a "user-level" requirement. The analyst first chooses the appropriate category of the new requirement in the nomenclature, from which they discover the generic element(s). The specific R2F elements, which are included in the scope of application of the new software and correspond to the category and generic elements of the new requirement, are then automatically extracted. The analyst chooses from among them the specific elements of the new requirement, either by adoption or by adaptation of the former to the new context. These are specific elements of similar requirements belonging to previous projects. If no choice is possible, the analyst then proceeds to create specific elements of the new requirement from scratch.

– In the second scenario, the SMART approach aims to support the elicitation process by reusing typical requirements (requirement patterns) to meet a "user-level" requirement. The analyst first chooses the appropriate category of the new requirement in the nomenclature, from which they obtain a list of typical requirements (requirement patterns) specific to the application area, which can be adapted as they wish to the new context, more particularly the specific elements.

7.2.2. *Specification activity*

We present a scenario that illustrates the use of the SMART approach in the specification activity: in this scenario, the SMART approach aims to support the specification process for a new "analyst-level" requirement. Considering the first elicitation scenario, a first draft can be generated on demand, according to the view corresponding to its category in the V6 requirements model. Analysts can then adopt this version or customize it according to the context of their project. Then, regardless of the elicitation scenario used, the new requirement is then added at the right place in the requirements document, in the appropriate module, according to the organization of the application domain of the new software, and then in the appropriate category, according to the organization of the nomenclature.

7.2.3. *Analysis activity*

We present three different scenarios that illustrate the use of the SMART approach in the analysis activity:

– In the first scenario, the SMART approach aims to support the completeness analysis process of the "user-level" and "analyst-level" requirements. First of all, R2F is automatically reduced to the specific elements, which fall within the new scope of application. The analyst can further refine it according to the context of the new software. The coverage rate of these elements by the "user-level" requirements, as well as the coverage rate of the latter by the "analyst-level" requirements, can then be automatically calculated. Therefore, the specific elements, which are not covered at all or not sufficiently, are highlighted in order to be considered in the elicitation of additional "user-level" requirements. Similarly, "user-level" requirements that are not covered at all or not sufficiently are highlighted in order to be taken into account in the elicitation of new "analyst-level" requirements.

– In the second scenario, the SMART approach aims to support the consistency analysis process of a given "analyst-level" requirement. Requirements for the same software, whose categories show a dependency on the category of the new requirement, and whose specific elements are the same as its own, are automatically extracted. The analyst can then manually analyze the consistency of the new requirement with the latter.

– In the third scenario, the SMART approach aims to support the analysis process of conflicts between a given "analyst-level" requirement and others. Requirements for the same software, whose categories conflict with the category of the new requirement, and whose specific elements are the same as its own, are automatically extracted. The analyst can then manually analyze the existence of conflicts between the new requirement and the latter.

7.2.4. *Validation activity*

We present a scenario that illustrates the use of the SMART approach in the validation activity: in this scenario, the SMART approach aims to support the validation process of a new "analyst-level" requirement against "user-level" requirements which allowed its derivation, and its other sources of information. All of these requirements and sources are automatically extracted based on the metadata: 5.1 Other requirement (5.1.1 Other requirement reference and 5.1.2 Relation type (derivation)) and 5.2 Source (5.2.1 Source reference and 5.2.2 Source type) of the RML-bis language. After this validation, the 2.2 Status life cycle metadata is set to "VALID".

7.2.5. *Qualification activity*

We present two different scenarios that illustrate how the SMART approach is used in the qualification activity:

– In the first scenario, the SMART approach aims to support the qualification process for a given "user-level" requirement. The qualification of this requirement by the RML-bis language is achieved through general metadata such as 1.1 Identifier and 1.3 Software project; traceability metadata such as 5.1 Other requirement (5.1.1 Other requirement reference and 5.1.2 Relation type), 5.2 Source (5.2.1 Source reference and 5.2.2 Source type), 5.4.1 Generic subject, 5.4.2 Specific subject, 5.5.1 Generic factor and 5.5.2 Specific factor; and taxonomy metadata such as 7.1 UA level, 7.2 BS2 level, 7.3 E2 level, 7.4 Nature, and 7.5 Application domain. These metadata are the first version of the requirement descriptor and will be used in the structured multi-criteria search for "user-level" requirements. They can later be supplemented with other metadata as needed.

– In the second scenario, the SMART approach aims to support the relationship qualification process of a given "user-level" or "analyst-level" requirement with the other requirements and development artifacts by using the following metadata: 5.1 Other requirement (5.1.1 Other requirement reference and 5.1.2 Relation type) and 5.3 Design artifact (5.3.1 Artifact reference and 5.3.2 Artifact type) of the RML-bis language.

8

Evaluation

The objective of this chapter is to evaluate the new SMART approach through comparison with the main existing approaches.

We analyze its respective adequacy with these different approaches through the tables that follow.

We show how this new approach reconsiders all existing categories by adopting, adapting or extending them to new categories.

8.1. Comparison with Somerville's approach

Table 8.1 compares SMART with Somerville's approach (Somerville 2016).

We note that in SMART, the concept of "system requirement" has been replaced by "analyst requirement" as opposed to "user requirement" (role-based categorization).

In addition, the concepts of "functional requirement" and "non-functional requirement" have been extended, respectively, to the concepts of "endogenous requirement" and "exogenous requirement".

Existing categories	Corresponding categories in SMART
User req.	User req.
System req.	Analyst req.
Domain req.	Endogenous req./software level req./operation req./cognitive context for operation req.: – concept definitions; – goal definitions; – business rule definitions.
Functional req.	Endogenous req./software level req./software req./functional req.
Non-functional req.	Exogenous req./software level req.
Performance req.	Exogenous req./software level req./quality req./performance req.
Usability req.	Exogenous req./software level req./quality req./usability req.
Security req.	Exogenous req./software level req./quality req./security req.
Reliability req.	Exogenous req./software level req./quality req./reliability req.
Operational process req.	Endogenous req./software level req./operation req./process support for operation req.
Development process req.	Endogenous req./software level req./development req./process support for development req.
Environmental req.	Endogenous req./software level req./operation req.: – human support for operation req.; – software support for operation req.; – hardware support for operation req.
Regulatory req.	Exogenous req./software level req./compliance req./law req.
Legislative req.	Exogenous req./software level req./compliance req./law req.
Ethical req.	Exogenous req./software level req./compliance req./law req.

Table 8.1. *Comparison with Somerville's approach*

8.2. Comparison with Lauesen's approach

Table 8.2 compares SMART with Lauesen's approach (Lauesen 2002). We consider that the "design" level in Lauesen's approach is a particular case of the software level in SMART, as explained in section 5.3.2. Therefore, the software-level requirements, which are considered to be design requirements, simultaneously relate to user interface, technical interface, function and data requirements. Their design aspect is due to the fact that they are expressed in terms of design elements such as screenshots for user interfaces, database schemas for data, algorithms for functions and finally communication protocols for technical interfaces.

Existing categories	Corresponding categories in SMART
Goal level req.	Business level req.
Domain level req.	System level req.
Product level req.	Software level req.
Design level req.	Endogenous req./software level req./software req: – user interface design req.; – technical interface design req.; – functional design req.; – data design req.
Managerial req.	Exogenous req./software level req./compliance req./management req.
Other deliverables	Exogenous req./software level req./compliance req./management req.
Quality req.	Exogenous req./software level req./quality req.
Functional req.	Endogenous req./software level req./software req./functional req.
Data req.	Endogenous req./software level req./software req./data req.

Table 8.2. *Comparison with Lauesen's approach*

8.3. Comparison with Robertson's approach

Table 8.3 compares SMART with Robertson's approach (Robertson et al. 2013). In SMART, Robertson's "look and feel requirements" category is considered to be dependent on the cultural factor.

Existing categories	Corresponding categories in SMART
Look and feel req.	Exogenous req./software level req./compliance req./culture req./look and feel req.
Usability req.	Exogenous req./software level req./quality req./usability req.
Performance req.	Exogenous req./software level req./quality req./performance req.
Operational and environmental req.	Endogenous req./software level req./operation req.: – software support for operation req.; – hardware support for operation req.
Maintainability and support req.	Exogenous req./software level req./quality req./maintainability req. Endogenous req./software level req./operation req.: – software support for operation req.; – hardware support for operation req.; – human support for operation req.
Security req.	Exogenous req./software level req./quality req./security req.
Cultural req.	Exogenous req./software level req./compliance req./cultural req.
Legal req.	Exogenous req./software level req./compliance req./law req.

Table 8.3. *Comparison with Robertson's approach*

8.4. Comparison with Van Lamsweerde's approach

Existing categories	Corresponding categories in SMART
Requirement	Endogenous req./software level req./software req.
Assumption	Endogenous req./software level req./operation req. Endogenous req./software level req./development req.
Domain property	Endogenous req./software level req./operation req./cognitive context for operation req./rule definition.
Definition	Endogenous req./software level req./operation req./cognitive context for operation req./concept definition.
Goal	Endogenous req./software level req./operation req./cognitive context for operation req./goal definition.

Table 8.4. *Comparison with Van Lamsweerde's approach*

Table 8.4 compares SMART with Van Lamsweerde's approach (Van Lamsweerde 2009). In SMART, all the concepts of Van Lamsweerde's approach have been grouped under the broad concept of endogenous requirement.

8.5. Comparison with Glinz's approach

Existing categories	Corresponding categories in SMART
Function	Endogenous req./software level req./software req./functional req.
Data	Endogenous req./software level req./software req./data req.
Performance	Exogenous req./software level req./quality req./performance req.
Specific quality	Exogenous req./software level req./quality req.
Constraint	Exogenous req./software level req./compliance req.

Table 8.5. *Comparison with Glinz's approach*

Table 8.5 compares SMART with Glinz's approach (Glinz 2007). In SMART, Glinz's different categories related to the "kind" facet have been replaced by the corresponding subcategories in the endogenous and exogenous categories. The three facets "representation", "role" and "satisfaction" have been replaced by new metadata from the RML language: the "representation" corresponds to metadata 4.2, the "role" facet corresponds to metadata 4.3 and the "satisfaction" facet corresponds to metadata 4.4.

8.6. Comparison with Meyer's approach

Table 8.6 compares SMART with Meyer's approach (Meyer et al. 2019). All of Meyer's concepts have a correspondence in SMART, with the exception of:

– the five fundamental categories: "limit", "lack", "meta requirement", "justification", and "obstacle", which we do not consider requirements as such;

– the three derived categories: "obligation", "assumption" and "invariant" which are only translated by a categorization by nature of the fundamental "constraint" category.

Existing categories	Corresponding categories in SMART
Component	R2F/dimension 1/subject.
Goal	R2F/dimension 1/operation environment/cognitive context for operation/goal.
Behavior	R2F/dimension 1/software: – function; – user interface; – technical interface.
Task	R2F/dimension 1/software/development/process support for development/development activity.
Product	R2F/dimension 1/software/development/cognitive context for development/artifact.
Constraint	R2F/dimension 2/compliance.
Role	R2F/dimension 1/operation environment: – software support for operation; – hardware support for operation; – human support for operation; R2F/dimension 1/development environment: – software support for development; – hardware support for development; – human support for development.
Limit	None.
Lack	None.
Meta-requirement	None.
Actor	R2F/dimension 1/operation environment: – human support for operation. R2F/dimension 1/development environment: – human support for development.
Justification	None.
Responsibility	R2F/dimension 1/operation environment: – human support for operation. R2F/dimension 1/development environment: – human support for development.

Obstacle	None.
Functional behavior	R2F/dimension 1/software/function.
Non-functional behavior	R2F/dimension 2/quality.
Business rule	R2F/dimension 1/operation environment/cognitive context for operation/rule.
Physical rule	R2F/dimension 1/operation environment/cognitive context for operation/rule.
Engineering decision	R2F/dimension 1/operation environment/cognitive context for operation/rule.
Obligation	None.
Assumption	None.
Invariant	None.

Table 8.6. *Comparison with Meyer's approach*

Conclusion

In this book, we have approached software requirements from a holistic perspective in order to better understand their nature, structure and usage. On the one hand, we have therefore identified the subjects relating to the future software and its development and operation environments, which they ought to cover (requirements subjects), and, on the other hand, the quality factors that affect them, as well as the compliance factors with the various multidisciplinary environmental constraints, which condition them. Indeed, it is unacceptable for analysts to continue to ignore the natural complexity of the requirements, focusing in particular on the functional and non-functional needs of the software, often considering for the latter only software quality. Their resulting specifications thus present ambiguous and poorly structured content, which other developers and stakeholders often find difficult to use.

Current categorizations of software requirements suffer from a high degree of ambiguity and inconsistency, mainly due to the lack of a common and clear reference framework for defining relevant software elements and environmental factors. This book revolutionizes the traditional approach by proposing a new systemic approach to requirements categorization and modeling, called SMART (Systemic Approach to caTegorizing and Modeling Requirements). This novel systemic approach provides:

1) at the conceptual level, a new reference framework, finally departing with divergent interpretations, through precise definition of the elements of the software and the environmental factors. This framework provides an essential basis for all other components of this approach, a new definition of requirements, as well as a new hybrid categorization of requirements;

2) at the operational level, a new requirements metadata model and a new multi-view requirements model.

The SMART approach was designed to be an excellent reference in terms of definition, categorization, qualification, structuring and representation of requirements, both for staunch IT specialists and for professionals in other sectors such as business process management, organization and change management.

It takes into account all the requirement categories proposed by existing approaches, adopting them, adapting them or extending them to new categories.

By adopting this new approach, professionals will be able to improve the clarity, accuracy and relevance of their specifications, thus maximizing the success of their software projects.

Finally, we strongly recommend the integration of SMART into requirements engineering and management through its adoption by their different models, methods and techniques. To this end, we would like to indicate that a first prototype of a requirements management tool based on the SMART approach is under construction.

Appendix

Cards Relating to the Nomenclature of the Categories of Requirements

Card 1

Corresponding categories of requirements in Table 5.6:

- *Endogenous req./Business level req./Software req./Functional req.*
- *Endogenous req./Business level req./Software req./Data req.*
- *Endogenous req./Business level req./Software req./User interface req.*
- *Endogenous req./Business level req./Software req./Technical interface req.*

Corresponding view of the V6 model: *DB view*

Adapted version: The "software_name" software (should/shall/must) **ensure** the necessary (**Function/Data/User interface/Technical interface**) to **satisfy** the following **business goal**: "specific business goal_statement".

EXAMPLE. The "e-lib" software must **ensure** the necessary **function** to **satisfy** the following **business goal**: increase the turnover of book sales.

RML-bis descriptor:

1.1 Identifier: R1

4.2 Representation: Operational	4.3 Role: Prescriptive	4.4 Satisfaction: Soft
5.4.1 GS: Function		5.5.1 GF: N/A
7.1 UA level: Analyst	7.2 BS2 level: Business	7.3 E2 category: Endogenous
7.4 Nature: Functional	7.5 Application domain: Library	

Card 2

Corresponding categories of requirements in Table 5.6:

- *Endogenous req./Business level req./Operation req./Process support for operation req.*
- *Endogenous req./Business level req./Operation req./Human support for operation req.*
- *Endogenous req./Business level req./Operation req./Software support for operation req.*
- *Endogenous req./Business level req./Operation req./Hardware support for operation req.*
- *Endogenous req./Business level req./Development req./Process support for development req.*
- *Endogenous req./Business level req./Development req./Human support for development req.*
- *Endogenous req./Business level req./Development req./Software support for development req.*
- *Endogenous req./Business level req./Development req./Hardware support for development req.*

Corresponding view of the V6 model: *DB view*

Adapted version: The "software_name" software (should/shall/must) **require** the necessary (**Process/Human/Software/Hardware**) support for (**Operation/Development**) to **satisfy** the following **business goal**: "specific business goal_statement".

EXAMPLE. The "e-lib" software must **require** the necessary **human** support for **operation** to **satisfy** the following **business goal**: increase the turnover from book sales.

RML-bis descriptor:

1.1 Identifier: R2

4.2 Representation: Operational	4.3 Role: Prescriptive	4.4 Satisfaction: Soft
5.4.1 GS: Human support for operation		5.5.1 GF: N/A
7.1 UA level: Analyst	7.2 BS2 level: Business	7.3 E2 category: Endogenous
7.4 Category: People	7.5 Application domain: Library	

Card 3

Corresponding categories of requirements in Table 5.6:

- *Endogenous req./Business level req./Operation req./Cognitive context for operation req.*
- *Endogenous req./Business level req./Development req./Cognitive context for development req.*

Corresponding view of the V6 model: *DB view*

Adapted version: The "software_name" software (should/shall/must) **adopt** the necessary (**Concept/Goal/Rule**)/(**Architecture/Method/Technique/Artifact**) to **satisfy** the following **business goal**: "specific business goal_statement".

EXAMPLE. The "e-lib" software must **adopt** the necessary **rules** to **satisfy** the following **business goal**: increase the turnover from book sales.

RML-bis descriptor:

1.1 Identifier: R3

4.2 Representation: Operational	4.3 Role: Prescriptive	4.4 Satisfaction: Soft
5.4.1 GS: Rule		5.5.1 GF: N/A
7.1 UA level: Analyst	7.2 BS2 level: Business	7.3 E2 category: Endogenous
7.4 Nature: Cognitive	7.5 Application domain: Library	

Card 4

Corresponding categories of requirements in Table 5.6:

- *Endogenous req./System level req./Software req./Functional req.*
- *Endogenous req./System level req./Software req./Data req.*
- *Endogenous req./System level req./Software req./User interface req.*
- *Endogenous req./System level req./Software req./Technical interface req.*

Corresponding view of the V6 model: *DSy view*

Adapted version: The "software_name" software (should/shall/must) **ensure** the necessary (**Function/Data/User interface/Technical interface**) to **support** the following **operation activity**: "specific operation activity statement".

EXAMPLE. The "e-lib" software must **ensure** the necessary **data** to **support** the following **operation activity**: searching for a book in the catalog can be done on the basis of more or less accurate references.

RML-bis descriptor:

1.1 Identifier: R4

4.2 Representation: Operational	4.3 Role: Prescriptive	4.4 Satisfaction: Soft
5.4.1 GS: Data		5.5.1 GF: N/A
7.1 UA level: Analyst	7.2 BS2 level: System	7.3 E2 category: Endogenous
7.4 Nature: Data	7.5 Application domain: Library	

Card 5

Corresponding categories of requirements in Table 5.6:

- *Endogenous req./System level req./Operation req./Process support for operation req.*
- *Endogenous req./System level req./Operation req./Human support for operation req.*
- *Endogenous req./System level req./Operation req./Software support for operation req.*
- *Endogenous req./System level req./Operation req./Hardware support for operation req.*
- *Endogenous req./System level req./Development req./Process support for development req.*
- *Endogenous req./System level req./Development req./Human support for development req.*
- *Endogenous req./System level req./Development req./Software support for development req.*
- *Endogenous req./System level req./Development req./Hardware support for development req.*

Corresponding view of the V6 model: *DSy view*

Adapted version: The "software_name" software (should/shall/must) **require** the necessary (**Process/Human/Software/Hardware**) support for (**Operation/Development**) to **support** the following **operation activity**: "specific operation activity_statement".

EXAMPLE. The "e-lib" software must **require** the necessary **software** support for **development** to **support** the following **operation activity**: searching for a book in the catalog can be done on the basis of more or less accurate references.

RML-bis descriptor:

1.1 Identifier: R5

4.2 Representation: Operational | 4.3 Role: Prescriptive | 4.4 Satisfaction: Soft

5.4.1 GS: Software support for development | 5.5.1 GF: N/A

7.1 UA level: Analyst | 7.2 BS2 level: System | 7.3 E2 category: Endogenous

7.4 Nature: Technical | 7.5 Application domain: Library

Card 6

Corresponding categories of requirements in Table 5.6:

- *Endogenous req./System level req./Operation req./Cognitive context for operation req.*
- *Endogenous req./System level req./Development req./Cognitive context for development req.*

Corresponding view of the V6 model: *DSy view*

Adapted version: The "software_name" software (should/shall/must) **adopt** the necessary (**Concept/Goal/Rule**)/(**Architecture/Method/Technique/Artifact**) to **support** the following **operation activity**: "specific operation activity_statement".

EXAMPLE. The "e-lib" software must **adopt** the necessary **technique** to **support** the following **operation activity**: the search for a book in the catalog can be done on the basis of more or less accurate references.

RML-bis descriptor:

1.1 Identifier: R6

4.2 Representation: Operational	4.3 Role: Prescriptive	4.4 Satisfaction: Soft
5.4.1 GS: Technique		5.5.1 GF: N/A
7.1 UA level: Analyst	7.2 BS2 level: System	7.3 E2 category: Endogenous
7.4 Nature: Cognitive	7.5 Application domain: Library	

Card 7

Corresponding categories of requirements in Table 5.6:

- *Endogenous req./Software level req./Software req./Functional req.*

Corresponding view of the V6 model: *DSo view*

Adapted version: The "software_name" software (should/shall/must) **ensure** "**Function**" ["Function_name"], described as follows: ["Function_statement"].

EXAMPLE. The "e-lib" software must **ensure** the **function**: "customer delivery", described as follows: prepare the delivery of booksellers who are solvent or have already made their payments.

RML-bis descriptor:

1.1 Identifier: R7

4.2 Representation: Operational	4.3 Role: Prescriptive	4.4 Satisfaction: Soft
5.4.1 GS: Function	5.5.1 GF: N/A	
7.1 UA level: Analyst	7.2 BS2 level: Software	7.3 E2 category: Endogenous
7.4 Nature: Functional	7.5 Application domain: Library	

Card 8

Corresponding categories of requirements in Table 5.6:

- *Endogenous req./Software level req./Software req./Functional req./Design Functional req.*

Corresponding view of the V6 model: *DSo view*

Adapted version: The "software_name" software (should/shall/must) **ensure** **"Function"** ["Function_name"], described as follows: ["Function_statement"], according to the **model**: ["Function_model"].

EXAMPLE. The "e-lib" software must **ensure** the **function**: "New customer registration", according to the **model**: the sequence diagram of this function (in appendix).

RML-bis descriptor:

1.1 Identifier: R8

4.2 Representation: Operational	4.3 Role: Prescriptive	4.4 Satisfaction: Soft
5.4.1 GS: Function	5.5.1 GF: N/A	
7.1 UA level: Analyst	7.2 BS2 level: Software	7.3 E2 category: Endogenous
7.4 Nature: Functional	7.5 Application domain: Library	

Card 9

Corresponding categories of requirements in Table 5.6:

- *Endogenous req./Software level req./Software req./Data req.*

Corresponding view of the V6 model: *DSo view*

Adapted version: The "software_name" software (should/shall/must) **ensure** **"Data"** ["Data_name"], described as follows: ["Data_statement"].

EXAMPLE. The "e-lib" software must **ensure** the **data**: "book, customer, order, invoice", described as follows: book (title, authors, ISBN); customer (name, address, telephone, email address); order (date, book titles and quantities); invoice (date, book titles, price, quantities, amount).

RML-bis descriptor:

1.1 Identifier: R9

4.2 Representation: Operational	4.3 Role: Prescriptive	4.4 Satisfaction: Soft
5.4.1 GS: Data		5.5.1 GF: N/A
7.1 UA level: Analyst	7.2 BS2 level: Software	7.3 E2 category: Endogenous
7.4 Nature: Data	7.5 Application domain: Library	

Card 10

Corresponding categories of requirements in Table 5.6:

- *Endogenous req./Software level req./Software req./Data req./Design Data req.*

Corresponding view of the V6 model: *DSo view*

Adapted version: The "software_name" software (should/shall/must) **ensure** "**Data**" ["Data_name"], described as follows: ["Data_statement"], according to the **model**: ["Data_model"].

EXAMPLE. The "e-lib" software must **ensure** the **data**: "book, customer, order, invoice", according to the **model**: the relational schema of the database (in appendix).

RML-bis descriptor:

1.1 Identifier: R10

4.2 Representation: Operational	4.3 Role: Prescriptive	4.4 Satisfaction: Soft
5.4.1 GS: Data		5.5.1 GF: N/A
7.1 UA level: Analyst	7.2 BS2 level: Software	7.3 E2 category: Endogenous
7.4 Nature: Data	7.5 Application domain: Library	

Card 11

Corresponding categories of requirements in Table 5.6:

- *Endogenous req./Software level req./Software req./User Interface req.*

Corresponding view of the V6 model: *DSo view*

Adapted version: The "software_name" software (should/shall/must) **ensure** "**User interface**" ["User interface_name"], described as follows: ["User Interface_statement"].

EXAMPLE. The "e-lib" software must **ensure** the **user interface**: "detailed consultation of a book resulting from the search" described as follows: provide a detailed view of each sold book, consisting of its image, which the visitor can enlarge, its price and availability, comments from its readers (former customers), its detailed table of contents, as well as extracts from its chapters.

RML-bis descriptor:

1.1 Identifier: R11

4.2 Representation: Operational	4.3 Role: Prescriptive	4.4 Satisfaction: Soft
5.4.1 GS: User interface		5.5.1 GF: N/A
7.1 UA level: Analyst	7.2 BS2 level: Software	7.3 E2 category: Endogenous
7.4 Nature: Interface		7.5 Application domain: Library

Card 12

Corresponding categories of requirements in Table 5.6:

- *Endogenous req./Software level req./Software req./User Interface req./Design User Interface req.*

Corresponding view of the V6 model: *DSo view*

Adapted version: The "software_name" software (should/shall/must) **ensure** "**User Interface**" ["User interface_name"], described as follows: ["User Interface_statement"], according to the **model**: ["User Interface_model"].

EXAMPLE. The "e-lib" software must **ensure** the **user interface**: "reduced consultation of a book resulting from the search" according to the **model**: the screenshot (in appendix).

RML-bis descriptor:

1.1 Identifier: R12		
4.2 Representation: Operational	4.3 Role: Prescriptive	4.4 Satisfaction: Soft
5.4.1 GS: User interface		5.5.1 GF: N/A
7.1 UA level: Analyst	7.2 BS2 level: Software	7.3 E2 category: Endogenous
7.4 Nature: Interface		7.5 Application domain: Library

Card 13

Corresponding categories of requirements in Table 5.6:

- *Endogenous req./Software level req./Software req./Technical interface req.*

Corresponding view of the V6 model: *DSo view*

Adapted version: The "software_name" software (should/shall/must) **ensure "Technical interface"** ["Technical interface_name"], described as follows: ["Technical interface_statement"].

EXAMPLE. The "e-lib" software must **ensure** the **technical interface**: "exchange with the CRM (Customer Relationship Management) software" described as follows: the "e-lib" software needs specific information about the CRM software such as the solvency of a bookseller before proceeding with its delivery.

RML-bis descriptor:

1.1 Identifier: R13

4.2 Representation: Operational	4.3 Role: Prescriptive	4.4 Satisfaction: Soft
5.4.1 GS: Technical interface		5.5.1 GF: N/A
7.1 UA level: Analyst	7.2 BS2 level: Software	7.3 E2 category: Endogenous
7.4 Nature: Interface		7.5 Application domain: Library

Card 14

Corresponding categories of requirements in Table 5.6:

- *Endogenous req./Software level req./Software req./Technical interface req./Design Technical interface req.*

Corresponding view of the V6 model: *DSo view*

Adapted version: The "software_name" software (should/shall/must) **ensure "Technical interface"** ["Technical interface_name"], described as follows: ["Technical interface_statement"], according to the **model**: ["Technical interface_model"].

EXAMPLE. The "e-lib" software must **ensure** the **technical interface**: "exchange with the compatibility software (Customer Relationship Management)" according to the **model**: the communication protocol (in appendix).

RML-bis descriptor:

1.1 Identifier: R14		
4.2 Representation: Operational	4.3 Role: Prescriptive	4.4 Satisfaction: Soft
5.4.1 GS: Technical interface		5.5.1 GF: N/A
7.1 UA level: Analyst	7.2 BS2 level: Software	7.3 E2 category: Endogenous
7.4 Nature: Interface		7.5 Application domain: Library

Card 15

Corresponding categories of requirements in Table 5.6:

- *Endogenous req./Software level req./Operation req./Process support for operation req.*

Corresponding view of the V6 model: *DSo view*

Adapted version: The "software_name" software (should/shall/must) **require** "**Process support for operation**", described as follows: ["Process support for operation_statement"].

EXAMPLE. The "e-lib" software must **require process support for operation** described as follows: the purchase process begins with a bookseller's access to the "mylib" e-distributor's website, his/her possible registration, his/her connection and access to the online catalog. Electronic catalogs can be very large, hence the usefulness of a multi-criteria search for books. The search for a book in the catalog can be done on the basis of more or less accurate references. The bookseller places the chosen books in a virtual basket. They then visit a checkout page, where a delivery option is selected, such as the delivery time (1 day, 3 days, 1 week, etc.). Finally, a payment option is selected, such as the payment method (credit card, PayPal, check after billing, etc.). After verifying all the details, the bookseller submits the order.

RML-bis descriptor:

1.1 Identifier: R15

4.2 Representation: Declarative | 4.3 Role: Assumptive | 4.4 Satisfaction: Soft

5.4.1 GS: Process support for operation | 5.5.1 GF: N/A

7.1 UA level: Analyst | 7.2 BS2 level: Software | 7.3 E2 category: Endogenous

7.4 Nature: Procedural | 7.5 Application domain: Library

Card 16

Corresponding categories of requirements in Table 5.6:

- *Endogenous req./Software level req./Operation req./Human support for operation req.*

Corresponding view of the V6 model: *DSo view*

Adapted version: The "software_name" software (should/shall/must) **require "Human support for operation"**, described as follows: ["Human support for operation_statement"].

EXAMPLE. The "e-lib" software must **require human support for operation**, described as follows: three customer order agents; two customer billing agents; two CRM and PRM service agents; two inventory agents; one marketing agent; one CRM and PRM service manager; one sales department manager; one inventory department manager; one accountant; one application administrator; one database administrator, etc.

RML-bis descriptor:

1.1 Identifier: R16

4.2 Representation: Declarative	4.3 Role: Assumptive	4.4 Satisfaction: Soft
5.4.1 GS: Human support for operation		5.5.1 GF: N/A
7.1 UA level: Analyst	7.2 BS2 level: Software	7.3 E2 category: Endogenous
7.4 Nature: Procedural	7.5 Application domain: Library	

Card 17

Corresponding categories of requirements in Table 5.6:

- *Endogenous req./Software level req./Operation req./Software support for operation req.*

Corresponding view of the V6 model: *DSo view*

Adapted version: The "software_name" software (should/shall/must) **require "Software support for operation"**, described as follows: ["Software support for operation_statement"].

EXAMPLE. The "e-lib" software must **require software support for operation**, described as follows: potential operating systems: Windows, Linux; other software: Mycompta accounting software; documentation: online software help.

RML-bis descriptor:

1.1 Identifier: R17

4.2 Representation: Declarative 4.3 Role: Assumptive 4.4 Satisfaction: Soft

5.4.1 GS: Software support for operation 5.5.1 GF: N/A

7.1 UA level: Analyst 7.2 BS2 level: Software 7.3 E2 category: Endogenous

7.4 Nature: Technical 7.5 Application domain: Library

Card 18

Corresponding categories of requirements in Table 5.6:

- *Endogenous req./Software level req./Operation req./Hardware support for operation req.*

Corresponding view of the V6 model: *DSo view*

Adapted version: The "software_name" software (should/shall/must) **require "Hardware support for operation"**, described as follows: ["Hardware support for operation_statement"].

EXAMPLE. The "e-lib" software must **require hardware support for operation**, described as follows: servers, namely the database server and the application server; processing unit – 8th- to 10th-generation Intel®/Core i (7/9) series processor of 4 GHz or more, with 32–128 GB DIMM memory; hard disk: SSD 3 x 480 GB or more, with RAID X configuration; digital tape drive with the same capacity as the total disk space; 17' flat panel display with an integrated video card of 1 GB or more; A4 (210 mm × 297 mm), two-sided and A3, PCL6e or later and Postscript, 12–16 ppm, 600 dpi laser printer compatible with the operating system; DVD+/–RW; PC scanner, from leading brands (Canon, Futjitsu, Epson, Brother); network hardware – one or more network cards supported by the installed network, with a capacity of 100/1,000 Mbps for optimal performance; other digital equipment: bank smart card readers.

RML-bis descriptor:

1.1 Identifier: R18

4.2 Representation: Declarative | 4.3 Role: Assumptive | 4.4 Satisfaction: Soft

5.4.1 GS: Hardware support for operation | 5.5.1 GF: N/A

7.1 UA level: Analyst | 7.2 BS2 level: Software | 7.3 E2 category: Endogenous

7.4 Nature: Technical | 7.5 Application domain: Library

Card 19

Corresponding categories of requirements in Table 5.6:

- *Endogenous req./Software level req./Operation req./Cognitive context for operation req./Concept definitions*

Corresponding view of the V6 model: *DSo view*

Adapted version: The "software_name" software (should/shall/must) **adopt "Concepts"**, described as follows: ["Concepts_statement"].

EXAMPLE. The "e-lib" software must **adopt** the **concepts** described as follows: electronic contract – definition 1; data encryption – definition 2; commercial robots – definition 3; digital signature – definition 4.

RML-bis descriptor:

1.1 Identifier: R19

4.2 Representation: Declarative	4.3 Role: Assumptive	4.4 Satisfaction: Hard
5.4.1 GS: Concept		5.5.1 GF: N/A
7.1 UA level: Analyst	7.2 BS2 level: Software	7.3 E2 category: Endogenous
7.4 Nature: Cognitive	7.5 Application domain: Library	

Card 20

Corresponding categories of requirements in Table 5.6:

- *Endogenous req./Software level req./Operation req./Cognitive context for operation req./Goal definitions*

Corresponding view of the V6 model: *DSo view*

Adapted version: The "software_name" software (should/shall/must) **adopt** "**Goals**", described as follows: ["Goals_statement"].

EXAMPLE. The "e-lib" software should **adopt** the **goals** described as follows: get into the international market of online wholesale bookstores; create new sales opportunities; and expand sales from classic books to electronic books (e-books). In fact, since everything that can be digitized can be easily delivered online, the delivery of e-books has become a real success story. The advantages of e-books include: they can be read on multiple portable devices, including tablets; they make the search for books easier and less cumbersome for booksellers; they make it possible to reach more geographically dispersed booksellers; they make it possible to reach more business partners (publishing houses); they increase employee productivity; they provide 24/7 coverage; they reduce billing errors; accelerate processing; they reduce the length of the trading cycle; they improve service quality; they reduce storage costs by reducing storage levels; they reduce administrative costs by eliminating paper; they enable electronic data interchange (EDI) so as to receive orders from booksellers electronically, and send them electronic invoices, etc.

RML-bis descriptor:

1.1 Identifier: R20

4.2 Representation: Declarative	4.3 Role: Assumptive	4.4 Satisfaction: Hard
5.4.1 GS: Goal		5.5.1 GF: N/A
7.1 UA level: Analyst	7.2 BS2 level: Software	7.3 E2 category: Endogenous
7.4 Nature: Cognitive	7.5 Application domain: Library	

Card 21

Corresponding categories of requirements in Table 5.6:

- *Endogenous req./Software level req./Operation req./Cognitive context for operation req./Rule definitions*

Corresponding view of the V6 model: *DSo view*

Adapted version: The software "software_name" (should/shall/must) **adopt** "**Rules**", described as follows: ["Rules_statement"].

EXAMPLE. The "e-lib" software must **adopt** the **rules** described as follows: book price calculation formula - ....; price discount calculation formula - ....; tax calculation formula - ....

RML-bis descriptor:

1.1 Identifier: R21

4.2 Representation: Declarative	4.3 Role: Assumptive	4.4 Satisfaction: Hard
5.4.1 GS: Rule		5.5.1 GF: N/A
7.1 UA level: Analyst	7.2 BS2 level: Software	7.3 E2 category: Endogenous
7.4 Nature: Cognitive	7.5 Application domain: Library	

Card 22

Corresponding categories of requirements in Table 5.6:

- *Endogenous req./Software level req./Development req./Process support for development req.*

Corresponding view of the V6 model: *DSo view*

Adapted version: The "software_name" software (should/shall/must) **require "Process support for development"**, described as follows: ["Process support for development_statement"].

EXAMPLE. The "e-lib" software must **require process support for development**, described as follows: analysis, general design, detailed design, implementation, installation and testing.

RML-bis descriptor:

1.1 Identifier: R22

4.2 Representation: Declarative	4.3 Role: Assumptive	4.4 Satisfaction: Soft
5.4.1 GS: Process support for development		5.5.1 GF: N/A
7.1 UA level: Analyst	7.2 BS2 level: Software	7.3 E2 category: Endogenous
7.4 Nature: Procedural	7.5 Application domain: Library	

Card 23

Corresponding categories of requirements in Table 5.6:

- *Endogenous req./Software level req./Development req./Human support for development req.*

Corresponding view of the V6 model: *DSo view*

Adapted version: The "software_name" software (should/shall/must) **require "Human support for development"**, described as follows: ["Human support for development_statement"].

EXAMPLE. The "e-lib" software must **require human support for development**, described as follows: two analysts, one design architect, one design engineer, two programmers and one tester.

RML-bis descriptor:

1.1 Identifier: R23

4.2 Representation: Declarative	4.3 Role: Assumptive	4.4 Satisfaction: Soft
5.4.1 GS: Human support for development		5.5.1 GF: N/A
7.1 UA level: Analyst	7.2 BS2 level: Software	7.3 E2 category: Endogenous
7.4 Nature: People	7.5 Application domain: Library	

Card 24

Corresponding categories of requirements in Table 5.6:

- *Endogenous req./Software level req./Development req./Software support for development req.*

Corresponding view of the V6 model: *DSo view*

Adapted version: The "software_name" software (should/shall/must) **require "Software support for development"**, described as follows: ["Software support for development_statement"].

EXAMPLE. The "e-lib" software must **require software support for development**, described as follows: case tools: IBM Rose; IDE: Eclipse; programing language: Java and JSP-compatible services, current Java programming standards (CSS2, AJAX, Java and JavaScript).

RML-bis descriptor:

1.1 Identifier: R24

4.2 Representation: Declarative	4.3 Role: Assumptive	4.4 Satisfaction: Soft
5.4.1 GS: Software support for development		5.5.1 GF: N/A
7.1 UA level: Analyst	7.2 BS2 level: Software	7.3 E2 category: Endogenous
7.4 Nature: Technical	7.5 Application domain: Library	

Card 25

Corresponding categories of requirements in Table 5.6:

- *Endogenous req./Software level req./Development req./Hardware support for development req.*

Corresponding view of the V6 model: *DSo view*

Adapted version: The "software_name" software (should/shall/must) **require "Hardware support for development"**, described as follows: ["Hardware support for development_statement"].

EXAMPLE. The "e-lib" software must **require hardware support for development**, described as follows, a computer with: processing unit: 8th- to 10th-generation Intel ®/Core i (7/9) serial processor of 4 GHz or higher with 32 GB to 128 GB DIMMs; hard drive: 3 × 480 GB SSD or larger, with RAID X configuration; 17' flat panel display with an integrated video card of 1 GB or more; OS-compatible laser printer, A4 (210 mm × 297 mm), double-sided and A3, PCL6e or newer, and Postscript, 12–16 ppm, 600 dpi; DVD+/–RW; PC scanner.

RML-bis descriptor:

1.1 Identifier: R25

4.2 Representation: Declarative	4.3 Role: Assumptive	4.4 Satisfaction: Soft
5.4.1 GS: Hardware support for development		5.5.1 GF: N/A
7.1 UA level: Analyst	7.2 BS2 level: Software	7.3 E2 category: Endogenous
7.4 Nature: Technical	7.5 Application domain: Library	

Card 26

Corresponding categories of requirements in Table 5.6:

- *Endogenous req./Software level req./Development req./Cognitive context for development req./Architecture req.*

Corresponding view of the V6 model: *DSo view*

Adapted version: The "software_name" software (should/shall/must) **adopt** "**Architecture**" ["Architecture_name"], described as follows: ["Architecture_statement"].

EXAMPLE. The "e-lib" software must **adopt** the **architecture**: three-layer, described as follows: the first layer corresponds to the human–machine interface that will appear on the customer's machine with a web browser. The second layer corresponds to the various types of processing that will be supported by the application service. The third layer corresponds to the data storage that will be supported by the database server.

RML-bis descriptor:

1.1 Identifier: R26

4.2 Representation: Declarative	4.3 Role: Assumptive	4.4 Satisfaction: Hard
5.4.1 GS: Architecture		5.5.1 GF: N/A
7.1 UA level: Analyst	7.2 BS2 level: Software	7.3 E2 category: Endogenous
7.4 Nature: Cognitive	7.5 Application domain: Library	

Card 27

Corresponding categories of requirements in Table 5.6:

- *Endogenous req./Software level req./Development req./Cognitive context for development req./Method req.*

Corresponding view of the V6 model: *DSo view*

Adapted version: The "software_name" software (should/shall/must) **adopt "Method"** ["Method _name"], described as follows: ["Method _statement"].

EXAMPLE. The "e-lib" software must **adopt** the **method**: Design By Contract (DBC).

RML-bis descriptor:

1.1 Identifier: R27

4.2 Representation: Declarative	4.3 Role: Assumptive	4.4 Satisfaction: Hard
5.4.1 GS: Method		5.5.1 GF: N/A
7.1 UA level: Analyst	7.2 BS2 level: Software	7.3 E2 category: Endogenous
7.4 Nature: Cognitive	7.5 Application domain: Library	

Card 28

Corresponding categories of requirements in Table 5.6:

- *Endogenous req./Software level req./Development req./Cognitive context for development req./Technique req.*

Corresponding view of the V6 model: *DSo view*

Adapted version: The "software_name" software (should/shall/must) adopt "**Technique**" ["Technique_name"], described as follows: ["Technique_statement"].

EXAMPLE. The "e-lib" software must **adopt** the **technique**: prototyping.

RML-bis descriptor:

1.1 Identifier: R28

4.2 Representation: Declarative	4.3 Role: Assumptive	4.4 Satisfaction: Hard
5.4.1 GS: Technique		5.5.1 GF: N/A
7.1 UA level: Analyst	7.2 BS2 level: Software	7.3 E2 category: Endogenous
7.4 Nature: Cognitive	7.5 Application domain: Library	

Card 29

Corresponding categories of requirements in Table 5.6:

- *Endogenous req./Software level req./Development req./Cognitive context for development req./Artifact req.*

Corresponding view of the V6 model: *DSo view*

Adapted version: The "software_name" software (should/shall/must) **adopt** "**Artifact**" ["Artifact_name"], described as follows: ["Artifact_statement"].

EXAMPLE. The "e-lib" software must **adopt** the artifacts: use case diagram, class diagram, sequence diagram, state machine diagram and activity diagram.

RML-bis descriptor:

1.1 Identifier: R29

4.2 Representation: Declarative	4.3 Role: Assumptive	4.4 Satisfaction: Hard
5.4.1 GS: Artifact		5.5.1 GF: N/A
7.1 UA level: Analyst	7.2 BS2 level: Software	7.3 E2 category: Endogenous
7.4 Nature: Cognitive	7.5 Application domain: Library	

Card 30

Corresponding categories of requirements in Table 5.6:

- *Exogenous req./Business level req./Functional adequation req.*
- *Exogenous req./Business level req./Performance req.*
- *Exogenous req./Business level req./Interoperability req.*
- *Exogenous req./Business level req./Usability req.*
- *Exogenous req./Business level req./Reliability req.*
- *Exogenous req./Business level req./Security req.*
- *Exogenous req./Business level req./Maintainability req.*
- *Exogenous req./Business level req./Portability req.*

Corresponding view of the V6 model: *XB view*

Adapted version: The ("software_name" software)/("GS selected from R2F": "SS_name")/(should/shall/must) **ensure** the necessary **Functional/Adequation/Performance/Interoperability/Usability/Reliability/Security/Maintainability/Portability**" to **satisfy** the following **business goal** "specific business goal_statement".

EXAMPLE. The "e-lib" software must **ensure** the necessary **security** to **satisfy** the following **business goal**: the use of CRM and PRM depends on information from booksellers and other partners, such as publishers, to improve sales services. Thus, customers and partners of the "my-lib" e-distributor must know that their data are being collected; they must give their permission for the data to be collected; they have to know how the data are used and ensure that these data are not shared with other parties.

RML-bis descriptor:

1.1 Identifier: R31		
4.2 Representation: Qualitative	4.3 Role: Prescriptive	4.4 Satisfaction: Soft
5.4.1 GS: Software	5.5.1 GF: Security	
7.1 UA level: Analyst	7.2 BS2 level: Business	7.3 E2 category: Exogenous
7.4 Nature: Quality	7.5 Application domain: Library	

Card 31

Corresponding categories of requirements in Table 5.6:

- *Exogenous req./Business level req./Management req.*
- *Exogenous req./Business level req./Technology req.*
- *Exogenous req./Business level req./Economics req.*
- *Exogenous req./Business level req./Culture req.*
- *Exogenous req./Business level req./Social req.*
- *Exogenous req./Business level req./Politics req.*
- *Exogenous req./Business level req./Law req.*

Corresponding view of the V6 model: *XB view*

Adapted version: The ("software_name" software)/("GS selected from R2F": "SS_name") (should/shall/must) **ensure** the necessary "**Management/Technology/Economics/Culture/Social/Politics/Law**" to **satisfy** the following "specific business goal_statement" **business goal**.

EXAMPLE. The "e-lib" software must ensure the necessary **language** to **satisfy** the following **business goal**: the "mylib" e-distributor wants to expand its network of customers to Africa and Asia.

RML-bis descriptor:

1.1 Identifier: R32

4.2 Representation: Qualitative	4.3 Role: Prescriptive	4.4 Satisfaction: Soft
5.4.1 GS: Software	5.5.1 GF: Culture/Language	
7.1 UA level: Analyst	7.2 BS2 level: Business	7.3 E2 category: Exogenous
7.4 Nature: Compliance	7.5 Application domain: Library	

Card 32

Corresponding categories of requirements in Table 5.6:

- *Exogenous req./System level req./Functional adequation req.*
- *Exogenous req./System level req./Performance req.*
- *Exogenous req./System level req./Interoperability req.*
- *Exogenous req./System level req./Usability req.*
- *Exogenous req./System level req./Reliability req.*
- *Exogenous req./System level req./Security req.*
- *Exogenous req./System level req./Maintainability req.*
- *Exogenous req./System level req./Portability req.*

Corresponding view of the V6 model: *XSy view*

Adapted version: The ("software_name" software)/("GS selected from R2F": "SS_name") (should/shall/must) **ensure** the necessary **"Functional adequation/Performance/ Interoperability/Usability/Reliability/Security/Maintainability/Portability"** to **support** the following "specific operation activity_statement" **operation activity**.

EXAMPLE. The "e-lib" software must **ensure** the **necessary** security to **support** the following **operation activity**: the sales system must verify a customer's credit card or accept electronic payments for books, such as PayPal.

RML-bis descriptor:

1.1 Identifier: R33

4.2 Representation: Qualitative	4.3 Role: Prescriptive	4.4 Satisfaction: Soft
5.4.1 GS: Software	5.5.1 GF: Security	
7.1 UA level: Analyst	7.2 BS2 level: System	7.3 E2 category: Exogenous
7.4 Nature: Quality	7.5 Application domain: Library	

Card 33

Corresponding categories of requirements in Table 5.6:

- *Exogenous req./System level req./Management req.*
- *Exogenous req./System level req./Technology req.*
- *Exogenous req./System level req./Economics req.*
- *Exogenous req./System level req./Culture req.*
- *Exogenous req./System level req./Social req.*
- *Exogenous req./System level req./Politics req.*
- *Exogenous req./System level req./Law req.*

Corresponding view of the V6 model: *XSy view*

Adapted version: The ("software_name" software)/("GS selected from R2F": "SS_name") (should/shall/must) **ensure** the necessary "**Management/Technology/Economics/Culture/Social/Politics/Law**" to **support** the following "specific operation activity_statement" **operation activity**.

EXAMPLE. The "e-lib" software must **ensure** the necessary **delivery** to **support** the following **operation activity**: the bookseller chooses a delivery option such as the delivery time (1 day, 3 days, 1 week, etc.).

RML-bis descriptor:

1.1 Identifier: R34

4.2 Representation: Qualitative 4.3 Role: Prescriptive 4.4 Satisfaction: Soft

5.4.1 GS: Software 5.5.1 GF: Management/Delivery

7.1 UA level: Analyst 7.2 BS2 level: System 7.3 E2 category: Exogenous

7.4 Nature: Compliance 7.5 Application domain: Library

Card 34

Corresponding categories of requirements in Table 5.6:

- *Exogenous req./Software level req./Quality req./Functional adequation req.*

Corresponding view of the V6 model: *XSo view*

Adapted version: The ("software_name" software)/("GS selected from R2F": "SS_name") (should/shall/must) **ensure "Functional adequation**" as follows: "Functional adequation_statement".

EXAMPLE. The "e-lib" software must **ensure functional adequation** as follows: meet 98% of the explicit and implicit expectations of its users.

Fit criterion: Number of positive software validation tests equal to 98% of the overall number of tests (the goal of these tests is functional validation, not error detection).

RML-bis descriptor:

1.1 Identifier: R35

4.2 Representation: Quantitative	4.3 Role: Prescriptive	4.4 Satisfaction: Hard
5.4.1 GS: Software	5.5.1 GF: Functional adequation	
7.1 UA level: Analyst	7.2 BS2 level: Software	7.3 E2 category: Exogenous
7.4 Nature: Quality	7.5 Application domain: Library	

Card 35

Corresponding categories of requirements in Table 5.6:

- *Exogenous req./Software level req./Quality req./Performance req.*

Corresponding view of the V6 model: *XSo view*

Adapted version: The ("software_name" software)/("GS selected from R2F": "SS_name") (should/shall/must) **ensure "Performance"** as follows: "Performance_statement".

EXAMPLE. The "e-lib" software must **ensure performance** as follows: support more than 1,000 simultaneous connections.

Fit criterion: Number of simultaneous connections >1,000.

RML-bis descriptor:

1.1 Identifier: R36

4.2 Representation: Quantitative	4.3 Role: Prescriptive	4.4 Satisfaction: Hard
5.4.1 GS: Software	5.5.1 GF: Performance	
7.1 UA level: Analyst	7.2 BS2 level: Software	7.3 E2 category: Exogenous
7.4 Nature: Quality	7.5 Application domain: Library	

Card 36

Corresponding categories of requirements in Table 5.6:

- *Exogenous req./Software level req./Quality req./Interoperability*

Corresponding view of the V6 model: *XSo view*

Adapted version: The ("software_name" software)/("GS selected from R2F": "SS_name") (should/shall/must) **ensure** "**Interoperability**" as follows: "Interoperability_statement".

EXAMPLE. The "e-lib" software must **ensure interoperability** as follows: the database should be standardized to be readable using free and open-source software.

RML-bis descriptor:

1.1 Identifier: R37

4.2 Representation: Qualitative	4.3 Role: Prescriptive	4.4 Satisfaction: Hard
5.4.1 GS: Software	5.5.1 GF: Interoperability	
7.1 UA level: Analyst	7.2 BS2 level: Software	7.3 E2 category: Exogenous
7.4 Nature: Quality	7.5 Application domain: Library	

Card 37

Corresponding categories of requirements in Table 5.6:

- *Exogenous req./Software level req./Quality req./Usability req.*

Corresponding view of the V6 model: *XSo view*

Adapted version: The ("software_name" software)/("GS selected from R2F": "SS_name") (should/shall/must) **ensure** "**Usability**" as follows: "Usability_statement".

EXAMPLE. The "e-lib" software must **ensure usability** as follows: at any time, the bookseller can consult contextual help pages, as well as execute a search through help pages. A guided tour will also have to be proposed to new visitors.

RML-bis descriptor:

1.1 Identifier: R38

4.2 Representation: Qualitative	4.3 Role: Prescriptive	4.4 Satisfaction: Hard
5.4.1 GS: Software	5.5.1 GF: Usability	
7.1 UA level: Analyst	7.2 BS2 level: Software	7.3 E2 category: Exogenous
7.4 Nature: Quality	7.5 Application domain: Library	

Card 38

Corresponding categories of requirements in Table 5.6:

- *Exogenous req./Software level req./Quality req./Reliability req.*

Corresponding view of the V6 model: *XSo view*

Adapted version: The ("software_name" software)/("GS selected from R2F": "SS_name") (should/shall/must) **ensure "Reliability"** as follows: "Reliability_statement".

EXAMPLE. The "e-lib" software must **ensure reliability** as follows: the average number of transactions between failures must be greater than 500,000, or the mean time between failures (MTBF) must be greater than 3 years.

RML-bis descriptor:

1.1 Identifier: R39

4.2 Representation: Quantitative	4.3 Role: Prescriptive	4.4 Satisfaction: Hard
5.4.1 GS: Software	5.5.1 GF: Reliability	
7.1 UA level: Analyst	7.2 BS2 level: Software	7.3 E2 category: Exogenous
7.4 Nature: Quality	7.5 Application domain: Library	

Card 39

Corresponding categories of requirements in Table 5.6:

- *Exogenous req./Software level req./Quality req./Security req.*

Corresponding view of the V6 model: *XSo view*

Adapted version: The ("software_name" software)/("GS selected from R2F": "SS_name") (should/shall/must) **ensure "Security"** as follows: "Security_statement".

EXAMPLE. The "e-lib" software must **ensure security** as follows: the protection measures of the "mylib" e-distributor include encryption – data are sent in an encrypted manner to guarantee the security and confidentiality of the exchanges. Inputting of the credit card number by the customer must be carried out in a secure manner, by encrypting the HTTP transfer, through the SSL protocol, the storage of databases of former thieves and the sharing of information with other e-sellers.

RML-bis descriptor:

1.1 Identifier: R40

4.2 Representation: Qualitative	4.3 Role: Prescriptive	4.4 Satisfaction: Hard
5.4.1 GS: Software	5.5.1 GF: Security	
7.1 UA level: Analyst	7.2 BS2 level: Software	7.3 E2 category: Exogenous
7.4 Nature: Quality	7.5 Application domain: Library	

Card 40

Corresponding categories of requirements in Table 5.6:

- *Exogenous req./Software level req./Quality req./Maintainability req.*

Corresponding view of the V6 model: *XSo view*

Adapted version: The ("software_name" software)/("GS selected from R2F": "SS_name") (should/shall/must) **ensure "Maintainability"** as follows: "Maintainability_statement".

EXAMPLE. The "e-lib" software must **ensure maintainability** as follows: the maintenance time of the software per year does not exceed 1 day.

RML-bis descriptor:

1.1 Identifier: R41

4.2 Representation: Quantitative	4.3 Role: Prescriptive	4.4 Satisfaction: Hard
5.4.1 GS: Software	5.5.1 GF: Maintainability	
7.1 UA level: Analyst	7.2 BS2 level: Software	7.3 E2 category: Exogenous
7.4 Nature: Quality	7.5 Application domain: Library	

Card 41

Corresponding categories of requirements in Table 5.6:

- *Exogenous req./Software level req./Quality req./Portability req.*

Corresponding view of the V6 model: *XSo view*

Adapted version: The ("software_name" software)/("GS selected from R2F": "SS_name") (should/shall/must) **ensure "Portability"** as follows: "Portability_statement".

EXAMPLE. The "e-lib" software must **ensure portability** as follows: the "e-lib" software can be transferred from a Windows environment to Linux and vice versa.

RML-bis descriptor:

1.1 Identifier: R42

4.2 Representation: Declarative	4.3 Role: Prescriptive	4.4 Satisfaction: Hard
5.4.1 GS: Software	5.5.1 GF: Portability	
7.1 UA level: Analyst	7.2 BS2 level: Software	7.3 E2 category: Exogenous
7.4 Nature: Quality	7.5 Application domain: Library	

Card 42

Corresponding categories of requirements in Table 5.6:

- *Exogenous req./Software level req./Compliance req./Management req.*

Corresponding view of the V6 model: *XSo view*

Adapted version: The ("software_name" software)/("GS selected from R2F": "SS_name") (should/shall/must) **ensure "Management modality**" as follows: "Management modality_statement".

EXAMPLE. The "e-lib" software must **ensure training** as follows:

The recommended training modules are:

1) Database Administration: this module is intended for two pre-selected "mylib" computer technicians who will manage the "e-lib" application database. The training should cover:

- database installation
- physical structure of the Oracle DBMS
- database administration and optimization

2) Application Server Administration: this module targets two other selected "mylib" computer technicians responsible for maintaining and managing the application server used for the "e-lib" deployment. The training should cover:

- physical structure of the application server components
- application server administration and maintenance.

RML-bis descriptor:

1.1 Identifier: R43

4.2 Representation: Declarative	4.3 Role: Normative	4.4 Satisfaction: Hard
5.4.1 GS: Software	5.5.1 GF: Management/Training	
7.1 UA level: Analyst	7.2 BS2 level: Software	7.3 E2 category: Exogenous
7.4 Nature: Compliance	7.5 Application domain: Library	

Card 43

Corresponding categories of requirements in Table 5.6:

- *Exogenous req./Software level req./Compliance req./Technology req.*

Corresponding view of the V6 model: *XSo view*

Adapted version: The ("software_name" software)/("GS selected from R2F": "SS_name") (should/shall/must) **ensure "Technology modality"** as follows: "Technology modality_statement".

EXAMPLE. The "e-lib" software must **ensure trending** as follows: Web 2.0, Client-Server Computing and Web services.

RML-bis descriptor:

1.1 Identifier: R44

4.2 Representation: Declarative	4.3 Role: Normative	4.4 Satisfaction: Hard
5.4.1 GS: Software	5.5.1 GF: Technology/Trending	
7.1 UA level: Analyst	7.2 BS2 level: Software	7.3 E2 category: Exogenous
7.4 Nature: Compliance	7.5 Application domain: Library	

Card 44

Corresponding categories of requirements in Table 5.6:

- *Exogenous req./Software level req./Compliance req./Economics req.*

Corresponding view of the V6 model: *XSo view*

Adapted version: The ("software_name" software)/("GS selected from R2F": "SS_name") (should/shall/must) **ensure "Economics modality"** as follows: "Economics modality_statement".

EXAMPLE. The "e-lib" software must **ensure cost** as follows: the development cost, including human, software and hardware support for development, must not exceed 10 million DZD.

RML-bis descriptor:

1.1 Identifier: R45

4.2 Representation: Quantitative	4.3 Role: Normative	4.4 Satisfaction: Hard
5.4.1 GS: Software	5.5.1 GF: Economics/Cost	
7.1 UA level: Analyst	7.2 BS2 level: Software	7.3 E2 category: Exogenous
7.4 Nature: Compliance	7.5 Application domain: Library	

Card 45

Corresponding categories of requirements in Table 5.6:

- *Exogenous req./Software level req./Compliance req./Culture req.*

Corresponding view of the V6 model: *XSo view*

Adapted version: The ("software_name" software)/("GS selected from R2F": "SS_name") (should/shall/must) **ensure "Culture modality"** as follows: "Culture modality_statement".

EXAMPLE. The "e-lib" software must **ensure ethics** as follows: the non-use of cookies without the consent of the bookseller.

RML-bis descriptor:

1.1 Identifier: R46

4.2 Representation: Declarative	4.3 Role: Normative	4.4 Satisfaction: Hard
5.4.1 GS: Software	5.5.1 GF: Culture/Ethic	
7.1 UA level: Analyst	7.2 BS2 level: Software	7.3 E2 category: Exogenous
7.4 Nature: Compliance	7.5 Application domain: Library	

Card 46

Corresponding categories of requirements in Table 5.6:

- *Exogenous req./Software level req./Compliance req./Social req.*

Corresponding view of the V6 model: *XSo view*

Adapted version: The ("software_name" software)/("GS selected from R2F": "SS_name") (should/shall/must) **ensure "Social modality"** as follows: "Social modality_statement".

EXAMPLE. The "e-lib" software must **ensure cooperation** as follows: several booksellers can cooperate in the same order to take advantage of quantity discounts.

RML-bis descriptor:

1.1 Identifier: R47

4.2 Representation: Declarative	4.3 Role: Normative	4.4 Satisfaction: Hard
5.4.1 GS: Software	5.5.1 GF: Social/Cooperation	
7.1 UA level: Analyst	7.2 BS2 level: Software	7.3 E2 category: Exogenous
7.4 Nature: Compliance e	7.5 Application domain: Library	

Card 47

Corresponding categories of requirements in Table 5.6:

- *Exogenous req./Software level req./Compliance req./Politics req.*

Corresponding view of the V6 model: *XSo view*

Adapted version: The ("software_name" software)/("GS selected from R2F": "SS_name") (should/shall/must) **ensure "Politics modality"** as follows: "Politics modality_statement".

EXAMPLE. The "e-lib" software must **ensure conflict resolution** as follows: any conflict must be resolved in a peaceful manner through dialog, putting the interest of the company above all other considerations. The parties most concerned by the software will have to be given preference.

RML-bis descriptor:

1.1 Identifier: R48

4.2 Representation: Declarative	4.3 Role: Normative	4.4 Satisfaction: Hard
5.4.1 GS: Software	5.5.1 GF: Politics/Conflict resolution	
7.1 UA level: Analyst	7.2 BS2 level: Software	7.3 E2 category: Exogenous
7.4 Nature: Compliance	7.5 Application domain: Library	

Card 48

Corresponding categories of requirements in Table 5.6:

- *Exogenous req./Software level req./Compliance req./Law req.*

Corresponding view of the V6 model: *XSo view*

Adapted version: The ("software_name" software)/("GS selected from R2F": "SS_name") (should/shall/must) **ensure "Law modality"** as follows: "Law modality_statement".

EXAMPLE. The "e-lib" software must **ensure legislation** as follows: the warranty of the "e-lib" software must cover a 3-year period of use (extendable) with a maintenance agreement as part of a service contract.

RML-bis descriptor:

1.1 Identifier: R49

4.2 Representation: Declarative	4.3 Role: Normative	4.4 Satisfaction: Hard
5.4.1 GS: Software	5.5.1 GF: Law/Legislation	
7.1 UA level: Analyst	7.2 BS2 level: Software	7.3 E2 category: Exogenous
7.4 Nature: Compliance	7.5 Application domain: Library	

References

Abran, A., Bourque, P., Dupuis, R., Tripp, L.L. (2004). *Guide to the Software Engineering Body of Knowledge*. IEEE Computer Society, Los Alamitos, CA [Online]. Available at: https://sceweb.sce.uhcl.edu/helm/SWEBOK_IEEE/SWEBOK_Guide_2004.pdf.

Abrial, J.R. (1996). *The B-Book – Assigning Programs to Meanings*. Cambridge University Press, Cambridge.

Aurum, A. and Wohlin, C. (2005). *Engineering and Managing Software Requirements*. Springer, New York.

Berners-Lee, T., Hendler, J., Lassila, O. (2001). The semantic web [Online]. Available at: https://www-sop.inria.fr/acacia/cours/essi2006/Scientific%20American_%20Feature%20Article_%20The%20Semantic%20Web_%20May%202001.pdf.

Berry, D.M. and Lawrence, B. (1998). Requirements engineering. *IEEE Software*, 25(2), 26–29.

Broy, M. (2018). Rethinking functional requirements: A novel approach – Categorizing system and software requirements. In *Software Technology: 10 Years of Innovation in IEEE Computer*, Hinchey, M. (ed.). John Wiley & Sons, New York.

Castillo, I., Losavio, F., Matteo, A., Bøegh, J. (2010). Requirements, aspects and software quality: The REASQ model. *Journal of Object Technology*, 9(4), 69–91.

Chaochen, Z., Hoare, C., Ravn, A. (1991). A calculus of durations. *Information Processing Letter*, 40(5), 269–276.

Chikh, A. (2017). Component-based approach for requirements reuse. *The Knowledge Engineering Review*, 32, E11. doi: 10.1017/S0269888917000030.

Dardenne, A., Van Lamsweerde, A., Fickas, S. (1993). Goal-directed requirements acquisition. *Science of Computer Programming*, 20, 3–50.

Davis, A.M. (1990). System testing: Implications of requirements specifications. *Information and Software Technology*, 32(6), 407–414.

Davis, A.M. (1993). *Software Requirements: Objects, Functions and States*. Prentice Hall, Hoboken.

Eckhardt, J. (2017). Categorizations of product-related requirements in practice: Observations and improvements. PhD Thesis, Universität München, Munich.

Fickas, S. and Helm, R. (1992). Knowledge representation and reasoning in the design of composite systems. *IEEE Transactions on Software Engineering*, 18(6), 470–482.

Gilb, T. (2005). *Competitive Engineering: A Handbook for Systems Engineering, Requirements Engineering and Software Engineering Management Using Planguage*. Butterworth-Heinemann, Oxford.

Glinz, M. (2005). Rethinking the notion of non-functional requirements [Online]. Available at: https://citeseerx.ist.psu.edu/document?repid=rep1&type=pdf&doi=beb907afd9cd2a2085107248a778733c08edd394.

Glinz, M. (2007). On non-functional requirements. In *Proceedings of the 15th IEEE International Requirements Engineering Conference (RE 2007)*, Delhi.

Gotel, O. and Finkelstein, A. (1994). An analysis of the requirements traceability problem. In *Proceedings of the 1st International Conference in Requirements Engineering*. IEEE, Colorado Springs, CO.

Haslhofer, B. and Klas, W. (2010). A survey of techniques for achieving metadata interoperability. *ACM Computing Surveys*, 42(2), 1–42.

Hood, C., Wiedemann, S., Fichtinger, S., Pautz, U. (2008). *Requirements Management: The Interface Between Requirements Development and All Other Systems Engineering Processes*. Springer, New York.

Hull, E., Jackson, K., Dick, J. (2017). *Requirements Engineering*. Springer, New York.

IEEE (1990). IEEE standard glossary of software engineering terminology (610.12). Working Document, IEEE, New York.

IEEE (1998). Standard for application and management of the systems engineering process. Working Document, IEEE, New York.

IEEE (2002). Draft standard for learning object metadata (1484.12.1-2002). Technical Report, IEEE, New York.

ISO/IEC (2006). Software engineering. Software product Quality Requirements and Evaluation (SQuaRE). Quality requirements (25030). Technical Standard, ISO, Geneva.

ISO/IEC (2007). Software engineering. Software product Quality Requirements and Evaluation (SQuaRE). Quality model and guide (CD 25010). Technical Standard, ISO, Geneva.

ISO/IEC/IEEE (2018). Systems and software engineering – Life cycle processes – Requirements engineering (29148). Technical Standard, ISO, Geneva.

Jacobson, I., Booch, G., Rumbaugh J. (1999). *The Unified Software Development Process*. Addison Wesley, London.

Jones, C.B. (1986). *Systematic Software Development Using VDM*. Prentice Hall, London.

Laplante, P.A. (2018). *Requirements Engineering for Software and Systems*, 3rd edition. Auerbach Publications, Boca Raton.

Lauesen, S. (2002). *Requirements: Styles and Techniques*. Addison-Wesley, London.

Lee, J. (1991). Extending the Potts and Bruns model for recording design rationale. In *Proceedings of the ICSE 13th International Conference on Software Engineering*. IEEE, Austin, TX.

McCall, J.A. and Matsumoto, M. (1980). Software quality metrics enhancements [Online]. Available at: https://apps.dtic.mil/sti/tr/pdf/ADA086985.pdf.

Meyer, B., Bruel, J.M., Ebersold, S., Galinier, F., Naumchev, A. (2019). Towards an anatomy of software requirements. In *Proceedings of the 51st International Conference, TOOLS 2019*, Innopolis. doi: 10.1007/978-3-030-29852-4_2.

Mordal, K., Laval, J., Ducasse S. (2011). Modèles de mesure de la qualité des logiciels. In *Évolution et rénovation des systèmes logiciels*, Seriai, A.-D. (ed.). Hermès Lavoisier, Paris.

Mylopoulos, J., Chung, L., Yu, E. (1999). From object-oriented to goal-oriented requirements analysis. *Communications of the ACM*, 42(1), 31–37.

OMG (2003). The unified modelling language version 2 [Online]. Available at: www.omg.org.

Paterno, F. and Faconti, G.P. (1992). *On the Use of LOTOS to Describe Graphical Interaction*. Cambridge University Press, Cambridge.

Pfleeger, C. and Pfleeger, S.L. (2006). *Security in Computing*, 4th edition. Prentice Hall, Hoboken.

Ramesh, B. and Jarke, M. (2001). Towards reference models for requirements traceability. *IEEE Transactions in Software Engineering*, 27(1), 58–93.

Robertson, S. and Robertson, J. (2013). *Mastering the Requirements Process – Getting Requirements Right*, 3rd edition. Addison Wesley, London.

Roques, P. (2008). *UML2. Modéliser une application web*. Editions Eyrolles, Paris.

Somerville, I. (2016). *Software Engineering*. Pearson Education, Harlow.

Spivey, J.M. (1989). *The Z Notation: A Reference Manual*. Prentice Hall, Hoboken.

Turban, E., King, D., Lee, J.K., Liang, T.P., Turban, D. (2015). *Electronic Commerce: A Managerial and Social Networks Perspective*. Pearson, London.

Van Lamsweerde, A. (2001). Goal-oriented requirements engineering: A guided tour. In *Proceedings of the 5th International Symposium on Requirements Engineering (RE'01)*. IEEE, Toronto.

Van Lamsweerde, A. (2009). *Requirements Engineering – From System Goals to UML Models to Software Specifications*. John Wiley & Sons, New York.

Vanícěk, J. (2006). Software quality requirements. *Agric. Econ.*, 52, 177–185 [Online]. Available at: https://www.agriculturejournals.cz/publicFiles/58017.pdf.

de Waal, B. (2016). The false dichotomy: Technical requirements versus business requirements [Online]. Available at: https://www.linkedin.com/pulse/false-dichotomy-technical-requirements-versus-business-de-waal.

Westfall, L. (2014). What, why, who, when, and how of software requirements. In *Handbook of Research on Emerging Advancements and Technologies in Software Engineering*, Ghani, I., Kadir, W., Ahmad, M. (eds). IGI Global, Pennsylvania.

Wiegers, K. and Beatty, J. (2013). *Software Requirements*. Microsoft Press, London.

Yu, E. (1993). Modelling organizations for information systems requirements engineering. In *Proceedings of RE'93 – 1st International Symposium on Requirements Engineering*. IEEE, San Diego, CA.

Yue, K. (1987). What does it mean to say that a specification is complete? In *Proceedings of the IWSSD-4, Fourth International Workshop on Software Specification and Design*. IEEE, Monterey, CA.

Zave, P. and Jackson, M. (1997). Four dark corners of requirements engineering. *ACM Transactions on Software Engineering and Methodology*, 6(1), 1–30.

Index

A, B

analyst, 53, 60, 61, 74, 81, 84, 87, 90, 92, 107, 109–111, 114, 123–170
approach, 4, 6, 43, 45, 47, 60, 64, 70, 74, 76, 77, 79, 87, 90, 92, 107–111, 113–117, 119, 121, 122
architecture, 54, 98, 125, 128, 148
artifact, 55, 83, 86, 87, 111, 118, 125, 128, 151
business, 3, 62, 65, 74, 75, 81, 84, 87, 91, 93, 100, 114, 115, 119, 122–125, 152, 153

C, D

CASE tools, 54, 146
categorization, 23–26, 32, 33, 40, 42, 43, 45, 47, 48, 60, 67, 73–77, 79, 80, 84, 88–90, 92, 107, 113, 117, 121, 122
  hybrid requirements, 48, 74, 79, 121
cognitive
  context, 48, 50–55, 68, 71, 73, 76, 77, 92, 93, 96–100, 114, 116, 118, 119, 125, 128, 141–143, 148–151
    for development, 54, 71, 73, 125, 128, 148–151
    for operation, 50, 51, 71, 73, 93, 100, 114, 116, 118, 119, 125, 128, 141–143
  requirements, 73
compliance, 56, 69, 71, 73, 84, 100, 114–118, 153, 155, 164–170
computer, 51, 54
concept, 7, 51, 96, 114, 116, 125, 128, 141
conceptualization, 47
culture, 57
data, 49, 65, 66, 70–72, 82, 91, 94, 115, 117, 123, 126, 131, 132
  requirements, 72
designer, 53
development
  activity, 53, 118
  environment, 48, 69, 71, 73, 83, 92–94, 100, 101, 118
digital device, 51, 54
documentation, 51

E, F

economics, 57
endogenous requirements, 67
environment
  development, 33, 53, 55, 73
  usage, 33, 49, 52

existing data, 50
exogenous requirements, 67
external actor, 50
factor, 7, 59, 68, 74, 75, 86, 90, 103–106, 115
  generic, 68, 86, 90
fit criterion, 89
function, 49, 65, 66, 70–72, 91, 94, 102, 117–119, 123, 126, 129, 130
functional, 70
  adequation, 56, 152, 154, 156
  requirements, 72

G, H

goal, 15, 19, 51, 62, 63, 65, 93, 94, 96, 100, 114–116, 118, 125, 128, 142
hardware support
  for development, 54, 71, 73, 118, 124, 127, 147
  for operation, 50, 51, 71, 73, 114, 116, 118, 124, 127, 140
human support
  for development, 53, 71, 73, 118, 124, 127, 145
  for operation, 49, 50, 71, 73, 114, 116, 124, 127, 138

I, L

IDE, 54, 146
interface requirements, 73
internal actor, 50
interoperability, 56, 70, 104, 152, 154, 158
law, 57
level
  analyst, 60
  business, 62
  conceptual, 121
  operational, 122
  software, 65
  system, 63
  user, 60
library, 54, 123, 125–128, 131–135, 138–149, 151–154, 156–170

M, N

maintainability, 56, 70, 116, 152, 154, 162
management, 57
method, 54, 125, 128, 149
networking, 51, 54

O, P

operating system, 50
operation
  activity, 50, 93, 101
  environment, 48, 49, 69, 71, 73, 83, 92–94, 100, 101, 118, 119
operationalization, 47, 79
other, 59
  developer, 53
  software, 50
  subject, 48
people requirements, 73
performance, 24, 35, 56, 70, 114, 116, 117, 152, 154, 157
politics, 57
portability, 56, 70, 152, 154, 163
process support
  for development, 53, 73
  for operation, 49, 50, 73
programmer, 53

Q, R

quality, 56, 69, 70, 73, 84, 100, 114–117, 119, 152, 154, 156–163
reference framework, 47, 59, 65, 79, 80, 84, 88

reliability, 56, 70, 114, 152, 154, 160
requirement(s), 7–12, 15–17, 20–22, 24–29, 34, 40, 59–61, 67–71, 74, 75, 85–90, 92, 95, 96, 102, 103, 109–111, 113, 117
  engineering, 10, 16, 21, 65, 79, 109, 121
  metadata model, 79, 122
rule, 51, 96, 116, 119, 125, 128, 143

S, T, U

security, 56, 70, 114, 116, 152, 154, 161
social, 57
  media, 51
software, 15, 16, 18, 19, 48–50, 53, 62, 65, 69–75, 81, 83, 84, 87, 91, 93, 94, 96, 98, 100–103, 114–119, 123, 124, 126, 127, 129–170
  support
    for development, 53, 71, 73, 118, 124, 127, 146
    for operation, 49, 50, 71, 73, 114, 116, 118, 124, 127, 139
subject, 11, 49–51, 53–55, 63, 66–68, 70, 72–75, 86, 90, 93, 94, 100–103
  generic, 67, 68, 86, 90
  specific, 67, 86
system, 15–19, 60, 62, 65, 74, 75, 81, 84, 87, 91, 93, 100, 114, 115, 126–128, 154, 155
systemic, 45, 121
technical, 118
  interface, 49, 50, 65, 66, 70, 71, 73, 91, 94, 115, 123, 126, 135, 136
  requirements, 73
technique, 55, 125, 128, 150
technology, 57
tester, 53
usability, 56, 70, 114, 116, 152, 154, 159
user, 15, 17, 19, 49, 60, 61, 65, 66, 70, 71, 73, 74, 81, 83, 84, 87, 90–92, 94, 102, 107, 109, 111, 114, 115, 118, 123, 126, 133, 134
  interface, 49, 65, 66, 70, 71, 73, 91, 94, 102, 115, 118, 123, 126, 133, 134

Other titles from

iSTE

in

Computer Engineering

2024

CHAKRABORTY Rajdeep, GHOSH Anupam, KUMAR MANDAL Jyotsna, CHOUDHURY Tanupriya, CHATTERJEE Prasenjit
Smart Edge Computing: An Operation Research Perspective
(International Perspectives in Decision Analytics and Operations Research Set – Volume 2)

HOMÈS Bernard
Fundamentals of Software Testing (2nd edition, revised and updated)

JERBI Abdessalem
Discrete-Event Simulation: Concepts and Production in Arena

PRADHAN Devasis, KUMAR SAHU Prasanna, MYO TUN Hla, CHATTERJEE Prasenjit
Artificial and Cognitive Computing for Sustainable Healthcare Systems in Smart Cities
(International Perspectives in Decision Analytics and Operations Research Set – Volume 3)

2023

CHOUDHURY Tanupriya, KHANNA Abhirup, CHATTERJEE Prasenjit, UM Jung-Sup, BHATTACHARYA Abhishek
Blockchain Applications in Healthcare: Innovations and Practices (International Perspectives in Decision Analytics and Operations Research Set – Volume 1)

PAI G A Vijayalakshmi
A Textbook of Data Structures and Algorithms 1: Mastering Linear Data Structures
A Textbook of Data Structures and Algorithms 2: Mastering Nonlinear Data Structures
A Textbook of Data Structures and Algorithms 3: Mastering Advanced Data Structures and Algorithm Design Strategies

2022

HOMÈS Bernard
Advanced Testing of Systems-of-Systems 1: Theoretical Aspects
Advanced Testing of Systems-of-Systems 2: Practical Aspects

MEHTA Shikha, TIWARI Sanju, SIARRY Patrick, JABBAR M.A.
Tools, Languages, Methodologies for Representing Semantics on the Web of Things

SIDHOM Sahbi, KADDOUR Amira
Systems and Uses of Digital Sciences for Knowledge Organization (Digital Tools and Uses Set – Volume 9)

ZAIDOUN Ameur Salem
Computer Science Security: Concepts and Tools

2021

DELHAYE Jean-Loïc
Inside the World of Computing: Technologies, Uses, Challenges

HARDIN Thérèse, JAUME Mathieu, PESSAUX François, VIGUIÉ DONZEAU-GOUGE Véronique
Concepts and Semantics of Programming Languages 1: A Semantical Approach with OCaml and Python
Concepts and Semantics of Programming Languages 2: Modular and Object-oriented Constructs with OCaml, Python, C++, Ada and Java

MKADMI Abderrazak
Archives in The Digital Age: Preservation and the Right to be Forgotten (Digital Tools and Uses Set – Volume 8)

TOKLU Yusuf Cengiz, BEKDAŞ Gebrail, NIGDELI Sinan Melih
Metaheuristics for Structural Design and Analysis (Optimization Heuristics Set – Volume 3)

2020

DARCHE Philippe
Microprocessor 1: Prolegomenes – Calculation and Storage Functions – Models of Computation and Computer Architecture
Microprocessor 2: Core Concepts – Communication in a Digital System
Microprocessor 3: Core Concepts – Hardware Aspects
Microprocessor 4: Core Concepts – Software Aspects
Microprocessor 5: Software and Hardware Aspects of Development, Debugging and Testing – The Microcomputer

DUVAUT Patrick, DALLOZ Xavier, MENGA David, KOEHL François, CHRIQUI Vidal, BRILL Joerg
Internet of Augmented Me, I.AM: Empowering Innovation for a New Sustainable Future

LAFFLY Dominique
TORUS 1 – Toward an Open Resource Using Services: Cloud Computing for Environmental Data
TORUS 2 – Toward an Open Resource Using Services: Cloud Computing for Environmental Data
TORUS 3 – Toward an Open Resource Using Services: Cloud Computing for Environmental Data

LAURENT Anne, LAURENT Dominique, MADERA Cédrine
Data Lakes
(Databases and Big Data Set – Volume 2)

OULHADJ Hamouche, DAACHI Boubaker, MENASRI Riad
Metaheuristics for Robotics
(Optimization Heuristics Set – Volume 2)

SADIQUI Ali
Computer Network Security

VENTRE Daniel
Artificial Intelligence, Cybersecurity and Cyber Defense

2019

BESBES Walid, DHOUIB Diala, WASSAN Niaz, MARREKCHI Emna
Solving Transport Problems: Towards Green Logistics

CLERC Maurice
Iterative Optimizers: Difficulty Measures and Benchmarks

GHLALA Riadh
Analytic SQL in SQL Server 2014/2016

TOUNSI Wiem
Cyber-Vigilance and Digital Trust: Cyber Security in the Era of Cloud Computing and IoT

2018

ANDRO Mathieu
Digital Libraries and Crowdsourcing
(Digital Tools and Uses Set – Volume 5)

ARNALDI Bruno, GUITTON Pascal, MOREAU Guillaume
Virtual Reality and Augmented Reality: Myths and Realities

CARDON Alain
Beyond Artificial Intelligence: From Human Consciousness to Artificial Consciousness

HOMAYOUNI S. Mahdi, FONTES Dalila B.M.M.
Metaheuristics for Maritime Operations
(Optimization Heuristics Set – Volume 1)

JEANSOULIN Robert
JavaScript and Open Data

PIVERT Olivier
NoSQL Data Models: Trends and Challenges
(Databases and Big Data Set – Volume 1)

SEDKAOUI Soraya
Data Analytics and Big Data

SALEH Imad, AMMI Mehdi, SZONIECKY Samuel
Challenges of the Internet of Things: Technology, Use, Ethics
(Digital Tools and Uses Set – Volume 7)

SZONIECKY Samuel
Ecosystems Knowledge: Modeling and Analysis Method for Information and Communication
(Digital Tools and Uses Set – Volume 6)

2017

BENMAMMAR Badr
Concurrent, Real-Time and Distributed Programming in Java: Threads, RTSJ and RMI

BOUHAÏ Nasreddine, SALEH Imad
Internet of Things: Evolutions and Innovations
(Digital Tools and Uses Set – Volume 4)

HÉLIODORE Frédéric, NAKIB Amir, ISMAIL Boussaad, OUCHRAA Salma, SCHMITT Laurent
Metaheuristics for Intelligent Electrical Networks
(Metaheuristics Set – Volume 10)

MA Haiping, SIMON Dan
Evolutionary Computation with Biogeography-based Optimization
(Metaheuristics Set – Volume 8)

PÉTROWSKI Alain, BEN-HAMIDA Sana
Evolutionary Algorithms
(Metaheuristics Set – Volume 9)

PAI G A Vijayalakshmi
Metaheuristics for Portfolio Optimization: An Introduction using MATLAB®
(Metaheuristics Set – Volume 11)

REYES-GARCIA Everardo
The Image-Interface: Graphical Supports for Visual Information
(Digital Tools and Uses Set – Volume 3)

REYES-GARCIA Everardo, BOUHAÏ Nasreddine
Designing Interactive Hypermedia Systems
(Digital Tools and Uses Set – Volume 2)

SZONIECKY Samuel, BOUHAÏ Nasreddine
Collective Intelligence and Digital Archives: Towards Knowledge Ecosystems
(Digital Tools and Uses Set – Volume 1)

2016

BLUM Christian, FESTA Paola
Metaheuristics for String Problems in Bio-informatics
(Metaheuristics Set – Volume 6)

DEROUSSI Laurent
Metaheuristics for Logistics
(Metaheuristics Set – Volume 4)

DHAENENS Clarisse, JOURDAN Laetitia
Metaheuristics for Big Data
(Metaheuristics Set – Volume 5)

LABADIE Nacima, PRINS Christian, PRODHON Caroline
Metaheuristics for Vehicle Routing Problems
(Metaheuristics Set – Volume 3)

LEROY Laure
Eyestrain Reduction in Stereoscopy

LUTTON Evelyne, PERROT Nathalie, TONDA Alberto
Evolutionary Algorithms for Food Science and Technology
(Metaheuristics Set – Volume 7)

MAGOULÈS Frédéric, ZHAO Hai-Xiang
Data Mining and Machine Learning in Building Energy Analysis

RIGO Michel
Advanced Graph Theory and Combinatorics

ZELM Martin, DOUMEINGTS Guy, MENDONÇA Joao Pedro
Enterprise Interoperability: in the Digitized and Networked Factory of the Future

2015

BARBIER Franck, RECOUSSINE Jean-Luc
COBOL Software Modernization: From Principles to Implementation with the BLU AGE® Method

CHEN Ken
Performance Evaluation by Simulation and Analysis with Applications to Computer Networks

CLERC Maurice
Guided Randomness in Optimization
(Metaheuristics Set – Volume 1)

DURAND Nicolas, GIANAZZA David, GOTTELAND Jean-Baptiste, ALLIOT Jean-Marc
Metaheuristics for Air Traffic Management
(Metaheuristics Set – Volume 2)

MAGOULÈS Frédéric, ROUX François-Xavier, HOUZEAUX Guillaume
Parallel Scientific Computing

MUNEESAWANG Paisarn, YAMMEN Suchart
Visual Inspection Technology in the Hard Disk Drive Industry

2014

BOULANGER Jean-Louis
Formal Methods Applied to Industrial Complex Systems
Formal Methods Applied to Complex Systems: Implementation of the B Method

EXPOSITO Ernesto, DIOP Codé
Smart SOA Platforms in Cloud Computing Architectures

GARDI Frédéric, BENOIST Thierry, DARLAY Julien, ESTELLON Bertrand, MEGEL Romain
Mathematical Programming Solver based on Local Search

KRICHEN Saoussen, CHAOUACHI Jouhaina
Graph-related Optimization and Decision Support Systems

LARRIEU Nicolas, VARET Antoine
Rapid Prototyping of Software for Avionics Systems: Model-oriented Approaches for Complex Systems Certification

LAURAS Matthieu, ZELM Martin, ARCHIMÈDE Bernard, BÉNABEN Frédérick, DOUMEINGTS Guy
Enterprise Interoperability: Interoperability for Agility, Resilience and Plasticity of Collaborations

OUSSALAH Mourad Chabane
Software Architecture 1
Software Architecture 2

QUESNEL Flavien
Scheduling of Large-scale Virtualized Infrastructures: Toward Cooperative Management

RIGO Michel
Formal Languages, Automata and Numeration Systems 1: Introduction to Combinatorics on Words
Formal Languages, Automata and Numeration Systems 2: Applications to Recognizability and Decidability

SAINT-DIZIER Patrick
Musical Rhetoric: Foundations and Annotation Schemes

TOUATI Sid, DUPONT DE DINECHIN Benoit
Advanced Backend Code Optimization

2013

ANDRÉ Etienne, SOULAT Romain
The Inverse Method: Parametric Verification of Real-time Embedded Systems

BOULANGER Jean-Louis
Safety Management for Software-based Equipment

DELAHAYE Daniel, PUECHMOREL Stéphane
Modeling and Optimization of Air Traffic

FRANCOPOULO Gil
LMF — Lexical Markup Framework

GHEDIRA Khaled
Constraint Satisfaction Problems: CSP Formalisms and Techniques

GOVAERT Gérard, NADIF Mohamed
Co-Clustering: Models, Algorithms and Applications

LANDRAGIN Frédérick
Man–Machine Dialogue: Design and Challenges

LUCAS Laurent, LOSCOS Céline, REMION Yannick
3D Video: Models, From Capture to Diffusion

ROCHANGE Christine, UHRIG Sascha, SAINRAT Pascal
Time-Predictable Architectures

WAHBI Mohamed
Algorithms and Ordering Heuristics for Distributed Constraint Satisfaction Problems

ZELM Martin, VAN SINDEREN Marten, FERRAIRA PIRES Luis, DOUMEINGTS Guy
Enterprise Interoperability: Research and Applications in the Service-oriented Ecosystem

2012

ARBOLEDA Hugo, ROYER Jean-Claude
Model-Driven and Software Product Line Engineering

BLANCHET Gérard, DUPOUY Bertrand
Computer Architecture

BOULANGER Jean-Louis
Industrial Use of Formal Methods: Formal Verification
Formal Methods: Industrial Use from Model to the Code

CALVARY Gaëlle, DELOT Thierry, SÈDES Florence, TIGLI Jean-Yves
Computer Science and Ambient Intelligence

MAHOUT Vincent
Assembly Language Programming: ARM Cortex-M3 2.0: Organization, Innovation and Territory

MARLET Renaud
Program Specialization

SOTO Maria, SEVAUX Marc, ROSSI André, LAURENT Johann
Memory Allocation Problems in Embedded Systems: Optimization Methods

2011

BICHOT Charles-Edmond, SIARRY Patrick
Graph Partitioning

BOULANGER Jean-Louis
Static Analysis of Software: The Abstract Interpretation

CAFERRA Ricardo
Logic for Computer Science and Artificial Intelligence

KORDON Fabrice, HADDAD Serge, PAUTET Laurent, PETRUCCI Laure
Distributed Systems: Design and Algorithms
Models and Analysis in Distributed Systems

LORCA Xavier
Tree-based Graph Partitioning Constraint

RIDHA MAHJOUB A.
Progress in Combinatorial Optimization: ISCO2010

TRUCHET Charlotte, ASSAYAG Gerard
Constraint Programming in Music

VICAT-BLANC Pascale, GOGLIN Brice, GUILLIER Romaric,
SOUDAN Sébastien
Computing Networks: From Cluster to Cloud Computing

2010

AUBRUN Christophe, SIMON Daniel, SONG Ye-Qiong
Co-design Approaches for Dependable Networked Control Systems

AUDIBERT Pierre
Mathematics for Informatics and Computer Science

BABAU Jean-Philippe, BLAY-FORNARINO Mireille, CHAMPEAU Joël,
ROBERT Sylvain, SABETTA Antonino
Model Driven Engineering for Distributed Real-Time Systems: MARTE modeling, model transformations and their usages

BOULANGER Jean-Louis
Safety of Computer Architectures

SIGAUD Olivier, BUFFET Olivier
Markov Decision Processes in Artificial Intelligence

MONMARCHÉ Nicolas, GUINAND Frédérick, SIARRY Patrick
Artificial Ants

SOLNON Christine
Ant Colony Optimization and Constraint Programming

2009

FOURNIER Jean-Claude
Graph Theory and Applications: with exercises and problems

GUÉDON Jeanpierre
The Mojette Transform: theory and applications

JARD Claude, ROUX Olivier H.
Communicating Embedded Systems: Software and Design

LECOUTRE Christophe
Constraint Networks: Techniques and Algorithms

2008

BANÂTRE Michel, MARRON Pedro Jose, OLLERO Anibal, WOLITZ Adam
Cooperating Embedded Systems and Wireless Sensor Networks

MERZ Stephan, NAVET Nicolas
Modeling and Verification of Real-time Systems: Formalisms and Software Tools

PASCHOS Vangelis Th
Combinatorial Optimization and Theoretical Computer Science: Interfaces and Perspectives

WALDNER Jean-Baptiste
Nanocomputers and Swarm Intelligence

2007

BENHAMOU Frédéric, JUSSIEN Narendra, O'SULLIVAN Barry
Trends in Constraint Programming

JUSSIEN Narendra
A to Z of Sudoku

2006

BABAU Jean-Philippe, CHAMPEAU Joël, GÉRARD Sébastien
From MDD Concepts to Experiments and Illustrations – DRES 2006

HABRIAS Henri, FRAPPIER Marc
Software Specification Methods: An Overview Using a Case Study

MURAT Cécile, PASCHOS Vangelis Th
Probabilistic Combinatorial Optimization on Graphs

PANETTO Hervé, BOUDJLIDA Nacer
Interoperability for Enterprise Software and Applications: Proceedings of the Workshops and the Doctorial Symposium of the Second IFAC/IFIP I-ESA International Conference: EI2N, WSI, IS-TSPQ 2006

2005

GÉRARD Sébastien, BABAU Jean-Philippe, CHAMPEAU Joël
Model Driven Engineering for Distributed Real Time Embedded Systems

PANETTO Hervé
Interoperability of Enterprise Software and Applications: Workshops of the INTEROP-ESA 2005 International Conference (EI2N, WSI, ISIDI and IEHENA 2005)

Printed and bound by CPI Group (UK) Ltd, Croydon, CR0 4YY
13/09/2026
14961011-0001